Pyjama Profit

The Millennial's Guide to a Sustainable Freelance Career

PYJAMA PROFIT

The Millennial's Guide to a Sustainable Freelance Career

Varun Mayya, Abhinav Chhikara

BLOOMSBURY
NEW DELHI • LONDON • OXFORD • NEW YORK • SYDNEY

BLOOMSBURY INDIA
Bloomsbury Publishing India Pvt. Ltd
Second Floor, LSC Building No. 4, DDA Complex, Pocket C – 6 & 7,
Vasant Kunj New Delhi 110070

BLOOMSBURY, BLOOMSBURY INDIA and the Diana logo are trademarks of Bloomsbury Publishing Plc

First published in India 2018
This edition published 2018

ISBN: TPB: 978-9-3871-4684-6; eBook: 978-9-3871-4685-3

2 4 6 8 10 9 7 5 3 1

Typeset in Arno Pro by Manipal Digital Systems
Printed in India by Gopsons Papers Pvt. Ltd., Noida

To the internet, without which we'd be working 9 to 5

CONTENTS

Preface
Pyjama Profit

"It is the ultimate luxury to combine passion and contribution. It's also a very clear path to happiness."

—Sheryl Sandberg

Why we wrote this book

To give you some background, I have worked in recruiting for over three years now, and the biggest factors that I've seen contribute to employability is **technical skill and presentation**. As a team, we've also seen an unprecedented shift in employer mindsets all over the world, and temporary staffing is at an all-time high.

When I was in college, I accidentally came across my first freelance project. It was a small website a friend of mine needed to be designed, but it threw me on a curiosity fueled path that opened big doors for me. I knew nothing about websites back then—I was a student who liked video games and did not know how to code. Both code and the internet were very daunting back then and it was the need to complete the project that required me to self-learn the coding languages needed to put together a website. In fact, I never wrote another line of code for at least a year after that—the entrepreneurial bug had hit me. Abhinav (my co-founder at the time, and co-author of this book) and I had started a t-shirt and merchandise company along with a few other friends in college. It was only a year later that we came full circle and started freelancing again.

We've seen thousands of developers, filmmakers, designers and digital marketers cap themselves by working in a 9-to-5 job—most of them blatantly ignorant of the wide variety of opportunities out there. Personally, it confused me that most of the advice given to young graduates was terrible. I understand the need for a 30-year-old with several years of experience in a particular space to stay bound to an industry and a company. But it surprised me that several 20-somethings were doing the same thing—essentially capping themselves to a salary bracket and a skill set.

After making everal thousands of dollars on the circuit and having worked for some amazing clients in remote teams across the world, a few of us got together to team up and build something in the recruitment space, while Abhinav went on to join Housing.com.

Jobspire, born out of that belief, went on to raise VC money and hire some of the brightest young minds in India. Now, we're armed with two years of hard recruitment data, having seen more than 4 million people visit our platform for a job and thousands of resumes uploaded. We thought it was time to put everything we knew into a book—to help youngsters and new grads understand that there are better paths in a country full of opportunities.

We envision this book to be a data-backed manual that every millennial in the country turns to when making his/her first career decision. A manual that is ready for the freelancing revolution on the horizon.

What this book is not

We wanted to have a section that clearly defines what this book is not:

1. This book is NOT an abstract rant about the freelance industry. We offer a perspective that might not be familiar

to you by including insights into our own personal learnings and earnings. We wanted to be open and upfront about what we made, and provide clear insights on how you can achieve the same, if not better income.

2. This book is NOT a replacement for hard work. We merely show you our paths and how we were able to learn what we learnt, and present ourselves the way we did. We made a ton of mistakes along the way, and hopefully this book will help you sidestep some of them. It still requires hard work and a dedicated approach for doing freelance.

If you're willing to put in the work, learn your core skill and apply what you've learnt, you should be able to see similar results. We've also kept the book as concise as possible, so you can head straight to work after this read.

We'd like to thank everyone mentioned in this book for helping us navigate the journey and for providing feedback on the early manuscript. A special thanks to Gaana Srinivas for helping us edit and refine the concepts in the book.

Chapter 1
Our Story

"If I'm going to tell a real story, I'm going to start with my name".

—**Kendrick Lamar**

Prologue

"Varun," my colleague said, pulling me out of my half-slumber.

"That's ₹30,000 in total".

Abhinav was counting crumpled notes of various denominations. We were five of us, sitting around a table under a shady red light in A-206, my apartment in Manipal. We called ourselves "SIZR", and our expertise back then was making t-shirts for our classmates. We would make custom t-shirts for each class in our batch, and we made a nice little profit of ₹15 a shirt. We had a supplier in Chennai who would print these t-shirts for us, and we would sell it at ₹300 a pop.

Everything from the logistics of taking orders to delivering door to door at the Manipal Institute of Technology hostels was handled by us. We never took a dime from any profits we made. Instead, we tried to pool the money to rent out a small 300 sqft. place for us to work from, and to pre-book future orders. We tried everything from making jersey-like class t-shirts with individual names on the back, to putting strontium aluminate (a substance with high photo-luminance) on t-shirts to try and make them glow in the dark (it worked!).

A year into it though, we weren't able to handle the sheer number of orders we were getting. Printing t-shirts takes an immense amount of effort per order. We were struggling with our five-member team to complete orders and ensure timely delivery. With exams around the corners, we weren't able to keep our customers happy.

We decided to abandon the idea of making t-shirts and spent every single rupee we made from the business buying ourselves courses in web design (I was interested in designing websites) and digital marketing. I have to this day maintained that my parents spent on my schooling, while I spent on my education.

Six months later, we were making websites, flyers and doing all sorts of digital odd jobs for friends and family. We were being paid anywhere between ₹700 to ₹2,000 per website ($10 to $30). We worked not for the money but because it was fun building things for others.

Swinging for the big leagues

One day, I stumbled upon oDesk (now called Upwork), an online platform for freelancers. I looked through some of the projects available, and the terminology used in most of those projects scared me. What in the world was "Bootstrap", "Foundation", "Laravel" and the 100+ other complicated words used by job posters in the web design section? I looked around for a simple web design project and found one that was listed with a budget of $100. The project description was simply "design a website for a Malaysian eye clinic". It was a weekend, and in a frenzy I decided to hit the apply button before I changed my mind.

oDesk immediately asked me to write a "cover letter". I didn't know what to write and at that point I was frightened by anything that involved money over the internet. So, being as honest as I could be, I wrote:

Dear Clinic Owner(Real name redacted),
I am a 19 year old who has been designing small time websites in HTML and CSS over the past year. I do not have the experience you stated as a requirement on the project, but I am willing to learn.
I believe I have an eye for design and have fairly decent communication skills.

Cheers,
Varun

(sic.)

Then I waited for three days.

On the fourth day, I received a reply, with my client telling me to connect with him on Skype.

After a one-hour conversation in which I told him I knew just the basics of website design, he finally told me that he liked my guts and offered me the project. I received a notification which I accepted.

"100$ for a website; how hard could it be?" I asked myself.

Two months later, I was still not done. The client kept asking for small changes. To me, each feature requested was something I didn't know anything about. I had to Google how to implement a particular thing, then read up on the examples and finally fiddle with codes myself until things clicked and the feature was live. On day seventy, I finally got paid—₹ 6,300 was credited to my bank account and I spent the entire thing on a Javascript course. I had found a way to make money online, and not the way you see in advertisements on torrent websites.

I learnt how to make money the legit way. Pic above: Ads on torrent sites trying to convince you that it's easy to make money posting and clicking on links.

I announced my $100 success to Kartik and the rest of the team and they were surprised, but also intimidated with the idea of working for someone else for money while still in college. Regardless, my "reckless" little team got cracking on oDesk, learning different skills. Abhinav decided to take graphic design and UI/UX projects, while Kartik took on more code-related projects. I took on a good mix of the two. After two years and working with multiple remote teams, all of us were familiar with very similar kinds of internet technology.

The funny thing is, internet technology also follows a selection process (like evolution follows natural selection). When some technology goes out of date, coders and designers switch to newer technology so employers are forced to upgrade too. If not for this quirk, we'd all have stuck to age-old technology and I'd never be able to land a freelance gig. Now I'm not saying there are no other benefits to upgrading technology, but if not for developers learning new skills, PHP (an old web development language) would still be the only language around.

All of us formed our own opinions on various things about the industry and our combined network was not just vast, it was also global. We were sharing projects, collaborating on some and going solo on the rest. The more confident our individual skill in doing something, the higher the likelihood we'd do it alone. Group projects were a good way for us to divide risk and learn things together.

Doing all of this while still in college was also burning us out. We were not sleeping too well, but our bank accounts were filled to the brim. The average SIZR billing rate rose to \$100–\$150 an hour, quite a distance from the \$100 I made over two months. As we were in college at that time, we didn't really save any money. I spent on courses and hardware, Kartik spent on books and Abhinav spent on travelling and getting his music app off the ground. Pravar, another friend who was part of SIZR, used the money to make more t-shirts for himself and Sandesh used his money on consoles and console games.

I have a firm belief that human beings gain confidence either by experience, or by learning very intimately from someone who has had that experience. We designed this book to not just be a good read but a roller-coaster experience based on our journey. When I encourage people to start freelancing, I remember saying some of these things: "You can have a better life." "It's not difficult to learn how to code." "You can work from home and make a better salary." "Yes, if you work hard enough and build a personal brand, it's probably more stable than a job."

You'll be surprised how most of these arguments fall flat. Humans do not make decisions based on the prospect of a future they cannot comprehend. How can you think you can have enough projects to run a family doing freelance work if you've never tried it before? The unknown is always scary.

In early 2013, I learnt a very good way to convince people to get started with freelancing.

Whenever I wanted someone to take up freelancing, I would carry my laptop, log in to my PayPal account, and show him or her my work history. That was all it took to get someone started on their freelancing journey.

The goal of this book is to prove that *making money in your pyjamas is not just possible but that it's easier than you think.*

Our own separate ways

After two years of freelancing, all of us loved working when we were together as a team, in a single room, even though we were working on our own projects. We had made nearly ₹30 lakh together (around $70k) by the end of the year, working a couple hours a day, including weekends. However, during the summer break that teamwork shattered and so did our motivation. We were sitting on the money we'd made and we were not able to spend anymore. We had no real needs and no family to support. So, instead of saving, we started working less. During summer break, Pravar and Sandesh had completely stopped freelancing to focus on biotechnology and film-making, respectively. The rest of us were still working on the odd project here and there. At this point, we were getting projects with ease, but the motivation to actually take one up and work on it was dwindling.

We all moved on to bigger things.

Kartik, Sandesh and I started Jobspire, a fun recruitment platform (which has seen more than 4 million people use it since we built it) and Abhinav moved on to start Lisn, a music app. Abhinav was also up to a lot of cool things—a start-up he worked with saw a small exit, he wrote a book on motion design and co-founded a music chat start-up that blew up. His new-found design skills enabled him to pursue a lot of random things to figure out what excited him. It was the end of a great journey for us but the beginning of a new, more challenging one.

Freelancing allowed us to work on exciting projects and make enough money to not just live our lives well, but also do things on the side we that were passionate about. Freelancing gave us means to an end. It gave us the freedom and money to work on the things we wanted and the confidence and exposure to take on bigger tasks. We know that whatever we do in the future, freelancing will always be a backup that will keep us afloat.

Tomorrow, if you put me in a strange country without any resources, all I need is a laptop and an internet connection and I know I'll build myself an awesome life fairly quick. I probably won't continue to freelance after I accumulate enough money because at that point my passions will drive my next project. This book is about how you can make the same kind of money and build the same kind of confidence. It's our best attempt at condensing all we've learnt into as small a book as possible.

Chapter 2

The Freelance Economy

"My favorite things in life don't cost any money. It's really clear the most precious resource we all have is time."

—Steve Jobs

Freelancing is the future

Today an increasing number of workers are leaving the traditional career path of joining an employer, grinding through the ranks and staying in one company for years. Surprisingly, these workers are driven less by the monetary reward and more by the ability to set their own schedules and pace. The average full-time freelancer works 5 to 10 hours less per week than the average employed worker and chooses when to take a break. Not only do they decide how much they want to work and when, but can also take full control of their income and lifestyle to do the things that matter to them.

Freelancers currently make up 35% of the American workforce. India has the second largest freelance economy, with over 15 million freelancers. The freelance workforce is the fastest-growing component of the current economy and this rise in the sheer number of freelancers compared to your parents' time can be attributed to the introduction of the internet. Before the internet, there was very little scope to learn skills by yourself and source opportunities from anywhere in the world. You were limited to your location and your current skill set. You could of course learn new skills, but you often had to be in the right place at the right time and have access to people who knew what you wanted to learn.

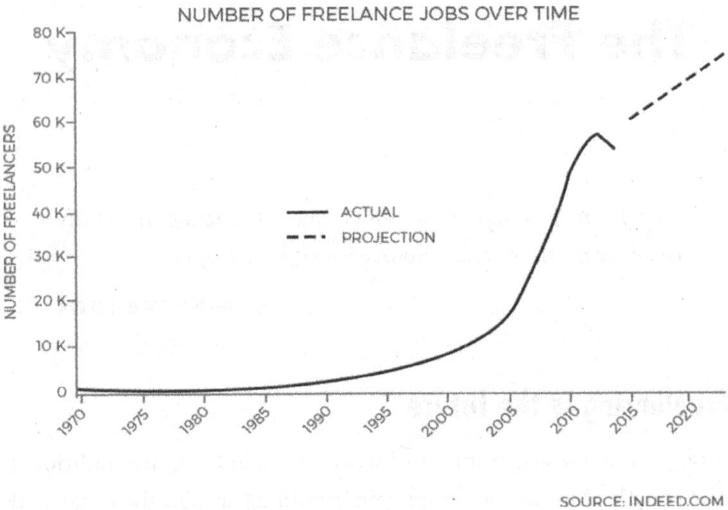

The number of freelance jobs online is only expected to increase

Today, you can find anything you want to learn online. Knowledge is available more freely than before. You can find the best teachers online, learn from the best universities. Several Ivy League colleges now host courses online—there's very little you can't learn on the internet! More importantly, the internet gives you visibility into a wide variety of options that you might not have known were available to you.

The only reason you'd need to join a college today is to meet interesting, smart people and get access to high-tech laboratories and equipment. When people ask me whether they should do a Master's degree, my answer is typically "depends on what you're majoring in".

For example, if you wanted to major in genetics, you'd need a high quality laboratory to conduct experiments and this is a solid case to actually go out and do a Master's in genetics. However, if you were learning marketing or sales, it makes more sense to learn online.

With a boom in online upskilling, there's also been a boom in the online freelance industry.

There are hundreds of websites you can sign up for and land freelance gigs. To give you an example, Upwork (formerly oDesk) is the world's biggest freelance platform, with projects worth $1B posted every year. Upwork gets somewhere between 30–40 million visitors on their site every month from every single country in the world. Only about 20% of this traffic is from the US, the rest is a long tail of countries with India, Philippines, Pakistan and Bangladesh at the top. The distribution is only natural, as supply follows demand. The most developed economies have a need for talent, and countries with this talent fill up the need.

The websites you will have most success with can depend on a bunch of factors, including your industry and skill level. We'll talk more about finding the right platform later in this book.

Why freelance works, regardless of your country

Conversion Rate

The simplest way to explain the benefits of the conversion rate is through something called the Big Mac Index. What it does is that it compares the prices of McDonald's Big Mac burger in different countries to get an idea for what the same item costs worldwide.

To give you an example, a Big Mac costs $1.6 in India, $4.2 in the US and $6.8 in Switzerland. It's a direct reflection of the purchasing power parity, i.e., $1 is not equal to $1 worldwide.

The Indian rupee is undervalued by 61%, which means we can buy goods for 61% less than Americans. This implies that $1 is worth around $0.4 in America. **So for doing equal work and getting equivalent pay given to an American worker, an Indian freelancer is actually earning 61% more.**

Let's take another example. In the US, a haircut costs, say, $20. In Uganda, it perhaps costs $2. In both cases, the same service is being provided but in the US it costs 10 times more. A loaf of bread costs $5 in America but just $0.5 in India. *Living in certain countries gives you better mileage per dollar,* put pure and simple.

As such, it's cheaper to hire a freelancer from a country where your money's worth more. Many companies look to outsource to freelancers to save money.

The Best Talent Isn't Always Local

Freelance allows companies access to a global market of talent. As a business owner, you might not have the talent you require in your local area. Hiring a freelancer prevents you from settling for a lower quality employee and reduces the overhead of relocating a person from another area to your locality.

Hiring freelancers also allows you to address specific needs with an expert. For example, you're planning to shift your website from one server to another but don't know how to do this. You can hire a freelance consultant who's an expert in this area specifically for this engagement and get their help without having to hire someone full time. Remember, hiring someone full time means to potentially pay the person for 12 months of work! For something that takes as little time as transferring some files from one server to the other, it makes no sense.

We're strong believers of the fact that full-time roles are dying – fewer small-to medium-sized businesses will have full-time roles. And even though hiring someone for an hour or two might be expensive, in the long run not having someone on the payroll can save an employer money, time and migraines.

The Pyjama Economy

To be honest, I've always loved the word "pyjama"—there's something so comforting in that word. On the other hand, I've always hated the word "economy". Even after starting multiple businesses, I'm still confused by the way it changes every few months. And it's not just me who can't pinpoint how the economy works – in fact, a blindfolded monkey was able to throw darts at a stock board and pick stocks that performed better than top ranked Wall Street brokers. In my own experience, I've met and hung out with guys who handle millions of dollars, but very few people know what is actually going on. If venture capitalists (VC) were that smart, every VC-backed start-up would make billions. The reality isn't that simple, and there are several factors that influence the success of a company.

When it comes to the online digital services economy, things are much more predictable. We have a reasonable understanding of what's working right now and we've seen it work over the years for ourselves and for several of our friends who've gone on to have successful freelance careers. Businesses will always want to hire the best people at a cost-effective rate, and the internet has enabled that at scale. The success of online platforms reflect that it's proven to work for a lot more people across the world.

Our experience with the freelance economy is a function of two things. First is having failed so many times that we can comfortably tell you what doesn't work. The second is having had enough successes in different projects to "guesstimate" what the best course of action in a given situation is.

Ten years ago, freelancing online was looked at as a way to make pocket money on the side. If you take a deep dive into the stats (Jobspire helps us keep up to date with what everyone's salary expectations are), you'll see that the **average freelancer in India**

makes more money in the same time period than a salaried employee for the same role. In fact, the ability to make more money means you work harder, which is an added benefit because this means that you can save up for a rainy day and take a break whenever you want. And if a project is really stressing you out, you can just drop it! In the corporate world, dropping a project isn't a very smart thing to do if you want to keep your job. In the freelance world, dropping your project is common practice. While you can quit in a real world corporate job, finding a new one is often a tiresome process.

The perception about online freelancing in India has usually been sweatshops and people in cyber cafes hurriedly writing codes before 8PM IST (when America begins its day) for meager hourly wages.

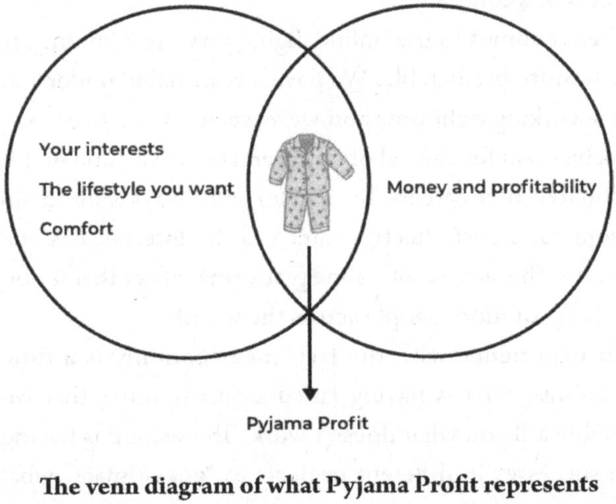

The venn diagram of what Pyjama Profit represents

Today, it represents the intersection of the things that drive you, the lifestyle you want to live and financial independence—a fantastic income, flexibility to work whenever and wherever and the ability to take a break at any time.

Online, there is no difference between you and someone from a different location. There are several freelancers from America, Spain and other first-world countries living comfortable lives with freelance income. Because there's no difference online, this means you can also make the same kind of money—dollar for dollar—as anybody else. If you wanted a job in New York, you'd need a visa, you'd need to find accommodation there, which is expensive, and your cost of living would shoot up. Imagine making the same kind of salary sitting at home with your loved ones.

Let's not forget the start-up boom that's been happening lately. With more smart individuals vying to build businesses online, there's more opportunity than ever for you to contribute.

Adding to these green pastures of opportunity is the ability to add your own creativity. Simply doing what you're told will make you money, but adding value and helping your clients with experience you've gained over your tenure as a freelancer is something they want today. Instead of just following orders, if you can tell your clients that some idea might not work because you've tried it before and it hasn't, it gives them more incentive to have you onboard for your experience.

So why is it easy for someone to make money online when everyone is complaining about not finding a job?

The answer is *small-to medium-sized businesses and business owners.* Let's take the example of a big company like Nestlé. They employ over 328,000 people across the world in different roles like management, production, finance, etc. Assuming most of these people work full time, they receive a fixed salary every month regardless of whether they work less or more. Of course, Nestlé, as a global conglomerate, has systems in place to make sure everybody works an even eight hours a day.

Now take the case of a business owner who sells something—say, lamp shades. Suppose they want to explore the option of finding customers online and selling directly to consumer through their website. What options do they have?

One option would be to hire a web developer full time. Depending on what part of the world they're in, this could cost thousands of dollars a year.

Another option would be to find someone with the skill needed and bring them onboard for one or two months and get it done.

How it would normally work is that they would ask their friends and network for recommendations and maybe also use an online platform like Upwork to post a job. They'd receive one or two recommendations from friends and maybe 40 to 60 applications online.

On Upwork, they're armed with detailed profiles, work history and samples of previous work to figure out who the best person for the job might be. They can make an informed decision, taking into consideration the level of quality they expect, the timeline, and their budget.

On successful completion, they leave a review online and let their friends know that they've worked with an amazing web developer. As a freelancer, this level of trust gets you more work, and over time also lets you increase your price, which lets you work toward the kind of projects that you are truly passionate about. The credibility you build allows you to gauge your own impact as a professional. This, in turn, leads to more clients interested in working with you, and the knowledge that you're going to have steady work allows you to really pick the kind of projects that interest you and charge accordingly for it.

The Economy and You

The economy seems like an abstract idea, but we'll try and simplify it for you.

Imagine you're sitting at a café. Every 10 minutes, somebody goes to the counter to pay for their coffee. There's lighting and air conditioning in this cafe, which costs them a certain amount of money every second. You're browsing Facebook on your phone and coming across ads that cost advertisers money for every view. Outside, there are cars waiting at a red light, burning fuel just by idling. There are vendors on the street selling snacks to passers-by.

The idea I'm trying to put in your head is that there is a flow of money around you every single day, every single second, wherever you are. It's like an invisible river flowing just above you. That's the economy.

Whenever you pay for something, you are adding to that flowing river. When you pay $4 for a coffee, you are saying that the coffee is worth $4 to you. The café that brewed the coffee gets the $4 in exchange for providing that value to you. They then pay maybe $1 to their suppliers, $0.5 to their barista and $0.3 towards their utility bill. They keep the profit and continue to run month after month. And so, the river flows.

That's how it works in real life, and that's exactly how it works on the internet. Businesses are spending money to make more money. They are spending on goods, suppliers, utilities, tools, labour, etc., which, in turn, is helping their businesses grow and make more money.

The amount of money you can take from this flowing river is the amount of value you can add to it. **You're free to take as much money as you want from this river; no limits. The only rule is that you have to put in value that is equal to or more than the money you take.**

When you understand and internalize this concept, you will start to see this pattern everywhere. The differences between a freelancer and full-time employee will also become clear to you.

As a full-time employee, you have a certain value to your company and the salary they're paying you reflects that. This value might change on a monthly basis but the money you make stays the same until you're promoted once every two years or so.

As a freelancer, there's no cap on the amount of money you can make, except maybe the number of hours you work in a day. If your work for a company can generate them an extra $X in revenue, they'd be glad to pay you to help them get there. The challenge then becomes figuring out what you can do for companies (**finding your value**), finding companies that need your skills (**communicating your value**) and how you do it with maximum impact (**delivering your value**). Those are the three things you need to figure out to have a successful freelance career.

1. Finding your value
2. Communicating your value
3. Delivering your value

A full-time employee and a freelancer both have 24 hours in a day. They both find something they're good at doing and provide that value to help a business make more money. The difference is that a freelancer can do as much or as little of it as they want, while a full-time employee is usually bound by the arbitrary limits their job imposes on them.

Chapter 3

Learning Your Core Skill

> *"It is so necessary to get the basic skills, because by the time you undergraduate or graduate, that field would have totally changed from your first day of school."*
>
> —**Leigh Steinberg**

Finding your value

In order for you to start making money freelancing, you need to have a skill set that is worth selling. The freelance market works the same way markets in real life work—there is a supply and demand ratio that is always in fragile balance. There's a demand for skills and professionals online, and finding your value comes down to meeting that demand.

Additionally, skills that are harder to learn will be scarcer in supply. This means that someone possessing them will be able to charge more.

I'm a huge believer of learning by doing. If you're starting out, you could take three to six months to get good at a skill, build up confidence, and then take up your first project. Or you could learn the basics of your skill in a week and start bidding for a project after that. You are paid to learn if you choose the latter.

You might wonder why would someone hire a newbie with questionable skills? Well, most people won't. But there are businesses out there that can't afford high prices, or simply can't justify a big investment on a freelancer. All that matters is that you have more skill than an average person, and boom, you've found your value. If you can design even a mediocre event poster for a business owner who doesn't have the skills to do it on their own and has only $20 to experiment with, you're delivering real value to them. Why not find that business owner and help them out? They get a better looking poster than they're used to, and you get your first project and a chance to apply your skills to something real. It's a win-win situation.

Here's what we've seen make money online. We're going to fondly call them the **Pyjama Categories** and rank them based on the time it takes to learn the basics, client demand and average billing rates. Client demand and average billing rates.

- Admin Support
- Marketing
- Content Writing
- Design
- Web Development
- Game Development and 3D Modelling
- Product Management
- App and Back-end Development

Later in this chapter, we'll dive deeper into each of these categories. Hopefully, you'll be able to find something that interests you.

The life cycle of a skill

Whenever new technology comes along, it is first adopted by a small number of enthusiastic users, and if it has merit, eventually trickles down to everyone. The same is true for skills and technologies you apply to servicing freelance clients.

Some clients might continue to use old technology because it's easier but several clients will switch to new technology because it usually allows them to move faster and build things more quickly. So despite the fact that there are freelancers with a lot more experience than you, you can make a good entry into the market by offering newer skills to clients. There will also be fewer freelancers with new skills, so they can usually bill higher rates and find clients with relative ease.

You'd be surprised at how many freelancers decide to stop learning because they are happy with their current project flow, skill set and billing rate. A positive attitude towards learning and picking up new skills goes a long way—especially when our skills tend to become outdated every few years—something we've learnt the hard way.

The Pyjama Categories have been selected keeping current and future demand in mind. Much like a typical adoption bell curve, each Pyjama Category goes through stages of **early adoption, acceptance, peak popularity, commoditization** and eventual **automation**. Your goal as a freelancer entering the market is to find a skill that is in it's peak popularity phase, or one that is in the early adoption or acceptance stages.

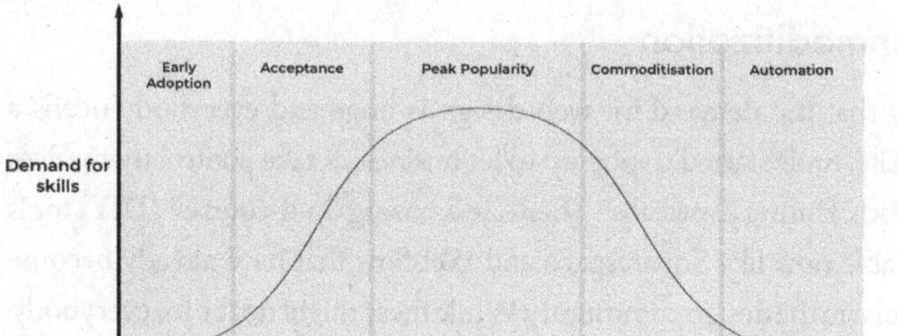

The Adoption Bell Curve applied to illustrate the life cycle of a skill

Let's take an example of one of these skills: web design.

Early Adoption

The early stages of a skill or an industry are marked by low awareness about it but high enthusiasm amongst the early adopters. In 1990, Tim Berners Lee invented the World Wide Web. Following this, web pages began to come up and more early adopters were attracted to this new technology.

Acceptance

Seeing the excitement amongst early adopters, entrepreneurs began to start creating commercial applications on the internet. This led to the initial public offering (IPO) boom towards the end of the 21st century as they created applications for everything imaginable and the frenzy led to overvalued start-ups.

Peak Popularity

After the boom, there was an inevitable bust in the early 2000s. However, over the next two decades, it became clear to everyone that the web was here to stay. As more consumers were coming online and getting comfortable with the internet, it made more and more sense for a business to be present online.

Commoditization

Now that the demand for web design is huge and everybody needs a website, tools started to pop up to let businesses take control themselves instead of hiring a specialist. There are amazing do-it-yourself (DIY) tools available now like Squarespace and Webflow that have already become popular in the design community. While these might not be for everybody, it shows that web design is on its way to becoming a commodity.

Automation

The next step after commoditization is naturally complete automation. Why rely on a human for something that a machine can do much better? There will of course be a demand for web design specialists and consultants at this point, but most of the heavy lifting will be automated.

Now keep in mind that while these stages apply to any skill worldwide, the rate at which these stages creep in varies from country to country. Businesses in developed countries might require these skills before those in developing countries. For example, businesses in the US knew the value of websites in the early 2000s, but in a country like India, that has only started in the past five years.

The Pyjama Categories

Let's get one thing straight; when you start freelancing, you are automatically in sales. You are effectively selling your skills and services and **you will be compared to** people selling their skills and services in the same price range. Much like a customer might pick one model of mobile phone over another because of a few features they might like, customers will pick one freelancer over the other not just based on their technical skill but also on brand name, past experience, presentation, certain quirks and a list of things that can be referred to as "gut feel".

The point I'm trying to make is that you don't just have to be good at what you do, but also at selling yourself.

We'll be going over each skill one by one and I'll try to outline what you should learn to enter the market and what background you'll need. We have recommended courses and learning material that we've taken ourselves and had a good experience with, but you're free to find resources online that best work for you. **Some of these are paid courses—we recommend always saving a little money from the freelance gigs that you do and using them for self-learning. This will ensure that you're always keeping up to date and investing in yourself.**

Pyjama Category	Time to Learn Basics	Client Demand	Billing Range/Hour	New Technology Cycles
Admin support	<1 month	Low	$3 to $10	1 to 3 years
Marketing	3 months	High	$15 to $300+	1 to 3 years
Content writing	4 weeks	High	$5 to $50+	2 to 5 years
Design	6 months	High	$10 to $250+	2 to 4 years
Web development	1 year	High	$10 to $300+	1 to 2 years
Game development and 3D modelling	6 months	High	$30 to $200+	3 to 4 years
Product management	1-4 years	High	$40 to $500+	3 to 6 months
App and back-end development	1 year	High	$20 to $600+	2 months to 4 years

Admin Support

Admin support roles are those that involve a lot of repetitive manual work, typically around data entry. It is considered the pioneer of online freelancing because it enabled millions of people in countries like India and Bangladesh who knew how to use Microsoft Excel to suddenly make more money on the side than they would in their day jobs. This job doesn't pay very well in India, or in a developed country like the US. But remember that Big Mac Index we were talking about? Suddenly, having a knowledge of data entry and an internet connection allowed people to start making US minimum wage instead of Indian minimum wage. A dollar an hour an hour suddenly jumped to $8 an hour – eight times the income they were previously making!

Some types of skills that fall under this Pyjama Category include transcription, data entry, personal and virtual assistantship, customer service and seb research.

Personally, I don't recommend this Pyjama Category today because of its low earning potential and high chance of automation. While data entry is a great supplementary skill to have and everyone must know a little Excel, it usually involves repetitive work that isn't fulfilling.

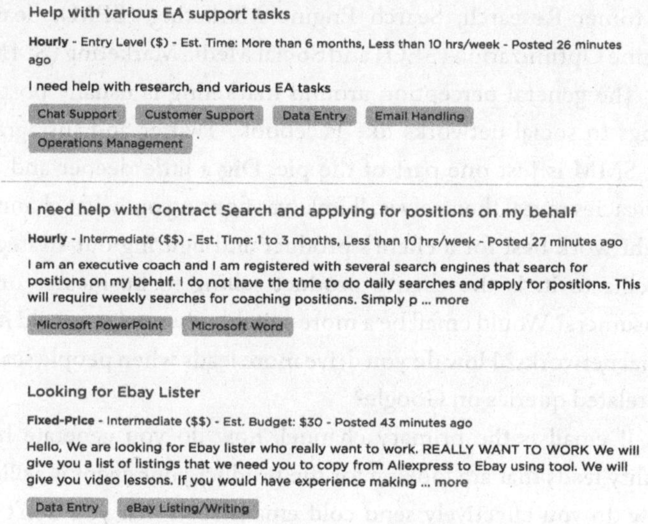

Examples of admin support projects on Upwork

If you're still interested, here are the resources you'll need:

Timeline	Course	Link
Within 1 month	Step-by-Step Spreadsheets for Absolute Beginners	https://www.udemy.com/step-by-step-spreadsheets-for-absolute-beginners/
Within 3 months	Become a Fast Typist in 14 Easy Steps	https://www.udemy.com/become-a-fastest-typist-in-14-easy-steps/
Within 6 months	Ultimate Excel Programmer Course	https://www.udemy.com/ultimate-excel-programmer/

Marketing

Digital marketing is today what computer programming was in 1999. It's the coolest new kid on the block with every business trying to get it right. This Pyjama Category includes Display Advertising, Email Marketing, Lead Generation, Market and Customer Research, Search Engine Marketing (SEM), Search Engine Optimization (SEO) and Social Media Marketing (SMM).

The general perception around marketing is usually posting things to social networks like Facebook, Twitter and Instagram. But SMM is just one part of the pie. Dig a little deeper and the intricacies reveal themselves. It involves figuring out what channels might work best for a client's product and figuring out strategies specific to it. Is the client's product selling to businesses or to consumers? Would email be a more suitable channel or would it be social networks? How do you drive more leads when people search for related queries on Google?

If email is the primary channel, how do you generate high quality leads that are looking for the product your client is selling? How do you effectively send cold emails such that you don't get marked spam? How do you create a funnel of leads eventually leading to sales of a product?

If social networks are the primary channel, what kind of content should you post? What, when and where should you post this content? How would you tweak paid campaigns to drive traffic to a page? Would paid campaigns on video content perform better as compared to text based content?

If search traffic is a primary channel, how do you optimize web pages to rank higher? Are blog posts effective in driving traffic or are longer case studies and whitepapers more effective? What keywords should you use? What call-to-actions should you add to content such that you can convert visitors to leads by capturing their email?

These are the questions you will need to grapple with daily, form hypotheses around and validate your assumptions.

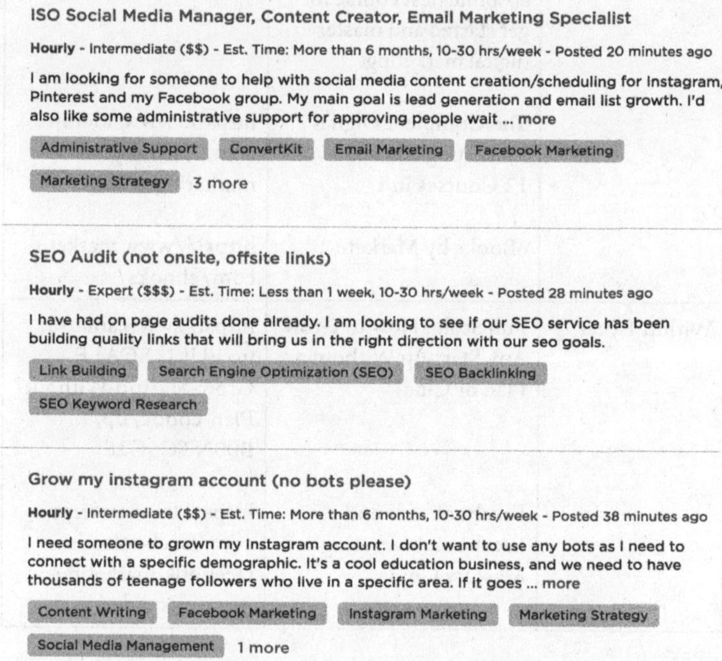

ISO Social Media Manager, Content Creator, Email Marketing Specialist

Hourly - Intermediate ($$) - Est. Time: More than 6 months, 10-30 hrs/week - Posted 20 minutes ago

I am looking for someone to help with social media content creation/scheduling for Instagram, Pinterest and my Facebook group. My main goal is lead generation and email list growth. I'd also like some administrative support for approving people wait ... more

Administrative Support | ConvertKit | Email Marketing | Facebook Marketing | Marketing Strategy | 3 more

SEO Audit (not onsite, offsite links)

Hourly - Expert ($$$) - Est. Time: Less than 1 week, 10-30 hrs/week - Posted 28 minutes ago

I have had on page audits done already. I am looking to see if our SEO service has been building quality links that will bring us in the right direction with our seo goals.

Link Building | Search Engine Optimization (SEO) | SEO Backlinking | SEO Keyword Research

Grow my instagram account (no bots please)

Hourly - Intermediate ($$) - Est. Time: More than 6 months, 10-30 hrs/week - Posted 38 minutes ago

I need someone to grown my Instagram account. I don't want to use any bots as I need to connect with a specific demographic. It's a cool education business, and we need to have thousands of teenage followers who live in a specific area. If it goes ... more

Content Writing | Facebook Marketing | Instagram Marketing | Marketing Strategy | Social Media Management | 1 more

Examples of marketing projects on Upwork

At Jobspire, we worked with several senior marketing executives. I learnt that digital marketing was mostly trial and error—some things work and some don't, and with experience you get a better feel of what works and what doesn't. There are a few basic techniques and tools that a marketer uses and with some expert help, here are the courses that I recommend:

Timeline	Course	Link
Within 3–6 months	Digital Marketing by General Assembly. If you can afford it, this is the absolute best course to get started and master digital marketing.	https://generalassemb.ly/education/digital-marketing
	The Complete Digital Marketing Course – 12 Courses in 1	https://www.udemy.com/learn-digital-marketing-course/
	eBooks by Marketo	https://www.marketo.com/ebooks/
Within 1 year	Full Scale: How to Grow Any Start-up Without a Plan or Clue	https://www.amazon.in/FULL-SCALE-Grow-Startup-Without-Plan-ebook/dp/B00NTC5G28
	Facebook Ads and Facebook Marketing Mastery Guide	https://www.udemy.com/facebook-ads-facebook-marketing-mastery-guide/

Content Writing

Over the course of running several businesses, I've hired over 200 people. At least 40 of them were content writers—an ode to the increasing demand for content and its effectiveness in driving organic traffic to a website. This Pyjama Category includes article and blog writing, academic writing and research, copywriting, creative writing, editing and proofreading, web content and so on.

As a freelance content writer, you have to understand the business and decide what content works best, how to convey the message in the best way possible and how to drive a point that will affect the business goal.

A company usually has an implicit set of beliefs and values in place, and good content aims to get that knowledge out into the world to become the voice of the business. When a business has an authentic voice, it attracts customers who share the same beliefs.

I would suggest not thinking of content writing purely as writing blog posts, but from the holistic lens of communication. While blog posts and articles are the most popular types of jobs available, written communication can have a wide reach in multiple channels. It involves generating ideas and then executing upon them.

To give you an example, you could be hired to write a blog post, the content for a website's home page, a company's values on a careers page, captions for social media campaigns, e-books and case studies for a business and so on.

Each of these projects is technically writing, but the intent and goal varies. The goal of the blog articles might be to drive more traffic and hence knowledge of SEO techniques will be valuable. The goal of the case studies might be to generate leads and hence you might have to research to get an in depth understanding of what potential customers might want.

The skill you have to develop is to distil the purpose and goal of the business and then to figure out how to communicate it to customers in the best way.

Often, you might also be asked to set up a Wordpress blog or to work within an existing team of content writers within a content management system (CMS) like Wordpress. Therefore, it also helps to get familiar with the tools and platforms you will be working with.

I need someone to write a business plan for my feature film for my investors.

Hourly - Expert ($$$) - Est. Time: Less than 1 week, Less than 10 hrs/week - Posted 12 minutes ago

I need help with final parts to my business plan. I have the budget, shooting schedule and sizzle reel. I need the sales pitch. The thing that will make them want to invest in the project. It's a low budget film with a budget of 2 million dollars ... more

Sales Writing

Article / Content writer for Website about Studying in Germany

Fixed-Price - Intermediate ($$) - Est. Budget: $150 - Posted 50 minutes ago

We help foreign students to come to Germany and choose the right German course and best universities. We need professional content writer for our website about studying in Germany. requirements: - professional writer - experience with seo oriented ... more

Academic Writing | Article Rewriting | Book Writing | Content Writing | Creative Writing | 4 more

---

Blog Writer

Fixed-Price - Entry Level ($) - Est. Budget: $30 - Posted 58 minutes ago

I am developing a local website that spotlights artists, creatives, and small businesses owners in my community. I am looking for writers who will conduct interviews and use other resources to write articles for the website. *Also able to do other va ... more

Article Writing | Blog Writing | Content Writing | Copywriting | Creative Writing | 5 more

Examples of content writing projects on Upwork

Timeline	Course	Link
Within 3 months	Content Is King: How to Write Killer Content for the Web	https://www.udemy.com/how-to-write-the-best-online-content/
Within 6–12 months	Complete Wordpress Training for Beginners	https://www.udemy.com/complete-wordpress-course-for-beginners/
	SEO (Search Engine Optimization) Basics	https://teamtreehouse.com/library/seo-basics
	Ninja Writing: The Four Levels of Writing Mastery	https://www.udemy.com/ninja-writing-the-four-levels-of-writing-mastery/

Design

This one is my favourite because it's how I started my freelance career. This Pyjama Category includes graphic design, user Interface and user experience design (UI/UX), web design, illustration, logo design and branding, presentations, video production, animation and so on.

That's a pretty wide net of skills, but we've included them under the same category because the boundaries between them are often fluid, with designers usually proficient in some combination of them.

The tools you would need to learn would depend on the exact work you're doing. Adobe Photoshop is the Swiss army knife that every designer needs to have familiarity with. It can handle almost anything you throw at it including logo design, presentations, web design, animations, 3D models etc.

Beyond Photoshop, there are a lot of tools specific to the kind of design work you will be doing. For example if you're working in UI/UX design, we would highly recommend Sketch App or Figma App. For logos and illustrations, vector design tools like Adobe Illustrator and Affinity Designer work well. For video production and animation, Adobe After Effects and Adobe Premiere Pro are widely used.

There are huge overlaps in what you can create with these tools. You can pick one of them to start with and move to others if the need arises, based on your specialization, projects and interests.

There is a lot more to design than just the tools, but we recommend starting with one of them to have a visual playground to play in. The theory of design and what the steps of a design process are, will be much easier to grasp once you have this foundation in place.

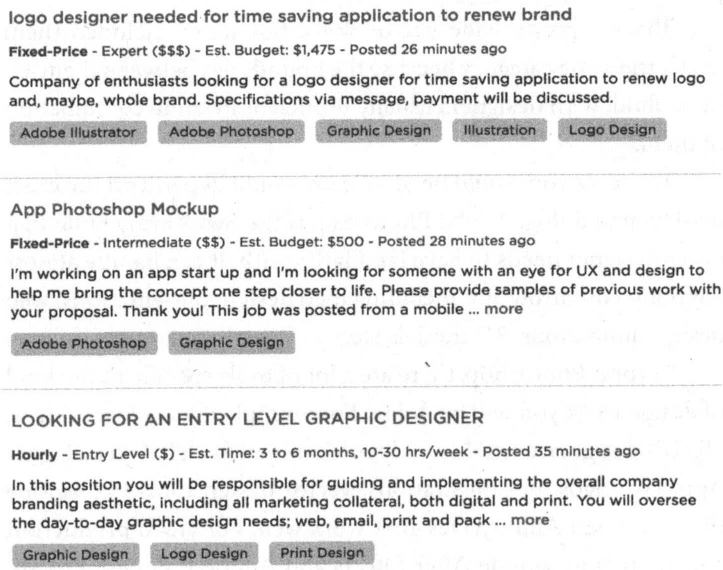
logo designer needed for time saving application to renew brand

Fixed-Price - Expert ($$$) - Est. Budget: $1,475 - Posted 26 minutes ago

Company of enthusiasts looking for a logo designer for time saving application to renew logo and, maybe, whole brand. Specifications via message, payment will be discussed.

Adobe Illustrator | Adobe Photoshop | Graphic Design | Illustration | Logo Design

App Photoshop Mockup

Fixed-Price - Intermediate ($$) - Est. Budget: $500 - Posted 28 minutes ago

I'm working on an app start up and I'm looking for someone with an eye for UX and design to help me bring the concept one step closer to life. Please provide samples of previous work with your proposal. Thank you! This job was posted from a mobile ... more

Adobe Photoshop | Graphic Design

LOOKING FOR AN ENTRY LEVEL GRAPHIC DESIGNER

Hourly - Entry Level ($) - Est. Time: 3 to 6 months, 10-30 hrs/week - Posted 35 minutes ago

In this position you will be responsible for guiding and implementing the overall company branding aesthetic, including all marketing collateral, both digital and print. You will oversee the day-to-day graphic design needs; web, email, print and pack ... more

Graphic Design | Logo Design | Print Design

Examples of design projects on Upwork

Timeline	Course	Link
Within 3 months	Udemy's Biggest and Most Popular Photoshop Course After Effects for Beginners	https://www.udemy.com/photoshoptraining/ https://www.udemy.com/aftereffects-beginners-complete/

Timeline	Course	Link
	Adobe Premiere Pro for Beginners	https://www.udemy.com/adobe-premiere-pro-video-editing/
	Switch to Sketch by Invision	https://www.switchtosketchapp.com/
	Mobile App Design in Sketch: UX and UI Design From Scratch	https://www.udemy.com/the-complete-design-course/
	Learn Figma App	https://learnux.io/course/figma
Within 6–12 months	Advanced Photoshop with Dave Cross	https://www.creativelive.com/courses/advanced-photoshop-techniques-dave-cross
	Adobe Illustrator Masterclass	https://www.udemy.com/illustrator-cc-masterclass/
	Design Lab's UI/UX courses	http://trydesignlab.com/?v=d
	iOS Human Interface Guidelines	https://elementary.io/docs/human-interfaceguidelines#humaninterface-guidelines
	Cooper Crash Course: Design Thinking in 3 Steps	https://www.udemy.com/cooper-crash-course/

Timeline	Course	Link
	2D Character Animation in After Effects Free Digital Painting Course by CtrlPaint Creating Icons with Purpose	https://www.udemy.com/2d-animation-with-no-drawing-skills/ https://www.ctrlpaint.com/ https://www.skillshare.com/classes/Icon-Design-Creating-Pictograms-with-Purpose/2139039143

Web Development

Web development has been one of the most popular and in-demand skills. This Pyjama Category includes web design and front-end development.

Web design involves designing web pages that effectively communicate the business' goal visually on a web page. There is an overlap here with the previous Pyjama Category, design because many freelancers start as web designers and gradually transition into web development. Sketch App and Figma App are currently two of the most popular web design tools available.

Web development involves programming web pages to be accessible on a web browser. While developing, you will have to think about how the website works across different browsers and different devices including mobile phones and tablets. You will also have to work with front-end frameworks and understand how to interface with databases and back-end languages.

You don't necessarily have to be good in design and development both, but doing so would definitely give you a competitive advantage.

We'd recommend doing both parts, getting well versed with the basics and finding your balance. Over time, you might realize that you enjoy one over the other, and you can diversify and niche down accordingly.

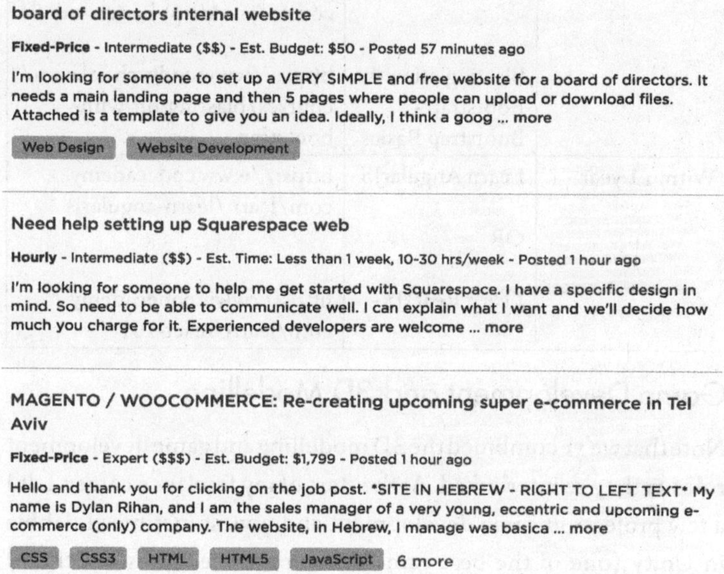

board of directors internal website

Fixed-Price - Intermediate ($$) - Est. Budget: $50 - Posted 57 minutes ago

I'm looking for someone to set up a VERY SIMPLE and free website for a board of directors. It needs a main landing page and then 5 pages where people can upload or download files. Attached is a template to give you an idea. Ideally, I think a goog ... more

Web Design | Website Development

Need help setting up Squarespace web

Hourly - Intermediate ($$) - Est. Time: Less than 1 week, 10-30 hrs/week - Posted 1 hour ago

I'm looking for someone to help me get started with Squarespace. I have a specific design in mind. So need to be able to communicate well. I can explain what I want and we'll decide how much you charge for it. Experienced developers are welcome ... more

MAGENTO / WOOCOMMERCE: Re-creating upcoming super e-commerce in Tel Aviv

Fixed-Price - Expert ($$$) - Est. Budget: $1,799 - Posted 1 hour ago

Hello and thank you for clicking on the job post. *SITE IN HEBREW - RIGHT TO LEFT TEXT* My name is Dylan Rihan, and I am the sales manager of a very young, eccentric and upcoming e-commerce (only) company. The website, in Hebrew, I manage was basica ... more

CSS | CSS3 | HTML | HTML5 | JavaScript | 6 more

Examples of web development projects on Upwork

Timeline	Course	Link
Within 3 months	HTML and CSS Basics	https://www.codecademy.com/learn/learn-html-css
	Switch to Sketch by Invision: Design Basics	https://www.switchtosketchapp.com/
	Figma for UX Design	https://www.lynda.com/Figma-tutorials/UX-Design-Tools-Figma/573133-2.html

Timeline	Course	Link
Within 6 months	Advanced HTML and CSS	http://learn.shayhowe.com/advanced-html-css/
	Javascript Basics	https://www.udacity.com/course/javascript-basics--ud804
	Blasting off with Bootstrap – Bootstrap Basics	https://www.codeschool.com/courses/blasting-off-with-bootstrap
Within 1 year	Learn AngularJS OR	https://www.codecademy.com/learn/learn-angularjs
	Learn ReactJS	https://www.codecademy.com/learn/react-101

Game Development and 3D Modelling

Note that we've combined the 3D modelling and game development roles as they're interlinked. At the start of my freelance career, I did a few projects in game development and now sometimes I dabble in Unity (one of the best game development engines out there) every so often to see how far it has come.

Currently, mobile games are the highest grossing category on the App Store and Play Store in terms of number of downloads worldwide, and this is expected to only increase as more people around the world switch to smartphones. With the massive success of the gaming industry and the advent of technology like virtual reality, learning how to make games has never been more rewarding. There are four parts to game development, each of which can spawn its own career map for you:

1. 3D model design (or alternatively, 2D sprite creation)
2. Level design
3. Game programming and scripting
4. Testing and quality assurance

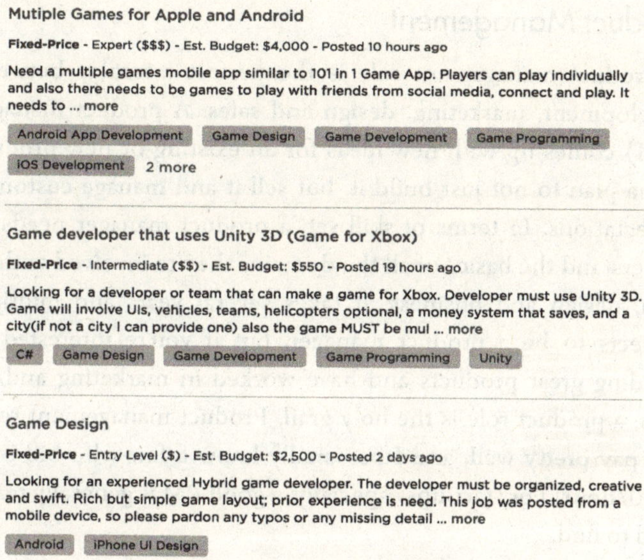

Mutiple Games for Apple and Android

Fixed-Price - Expert ($$$) - Est. Budget: $4,000 - Posted 10 hours ago

Need a multiple games mobile app similar to 101 in 1 Game App. Players can play individually and also there needs to be games to play with friends from social media, connect and play. It needs to ... more

Android App Development | Game Design | Game Development | Game Programming | iOS Development | 2 more

Game developer that uses Unity 3D (Game for Xbox)

Fixed-Price - Intermediate ($$) - Est. Budget: $550 - Posted 19 hours ago

Looking for a developer or team that can make a game for Xbox. Developer must use Unity 3D. Game will involve UIs, vehicles, teams, helicopters optional, a money system that saves, and a city(if not a city I can provide one) also the game MUST be mul ... more

C# | Game Design | Game Development | Game Programming | Unity

Game Design

Fixed-Price - Entry Level ($) - Est. Budget: $2,500 - Posted 2 days ago

Looking for an experienced Hybrid game developer. The developer must be organized, creative and swift. Rich but simple game layout; prior experience is need. This job was posted from a mobile device, so please pardon any typos or any missing detail ... more

Android | iPhone UI Design

Examples of game development projects on Upwork

Working with one of the best game designers from Ubisoft, we've come up with this list:

Timeline	Course	Link
Within 3 months	Learn to Code by Making Games — Complete C# Unity Developer	https://www.udemy.com/unitycourse/
Within 6 months	Learn Blender 3D Modeling for Unity Video Game Development Paladin Studios' Building Levels in Unity	https://www.udemy.com/learn-blender-3d-modeling-for-unity-video-game-development/ http://www.paladinstudios.com/2013/07/05/building-levels-in-unity-part-1-of-3/
Within 1 year	Advanced Unity: 3D Game Programming	https://www.lynda.com/Unity-3D-tutorials/Advanced-Unity-3D-Game-Programming/160270-2.html

Product Management

A product management role is the perfect interplay between development, marketing, design and sales. A product manager (PM) comes up with new ideas for an existing or new product and a plan to not just build it, but sell it and manage customer expectations. In terms of skill set, a product manager needs to understand the basics of all the domains they're involved with—tech, design and business. It takes several years and multiple projects to be a product manager, but if you're interested in building great products and have worked in marketing and/or tech, a product role is the holy grail. Product management roles can pay pretty well, and I personally know a few who bill over $300/hour! For start-ups especially, a good PM is generally really hard to find.

EXPERIENCED E-Commerce Product Manager Needed

Fixed-Price - Expert ($$$) - Est. Budget: $1,000 - Posted 2 hours ago

For a new e-commerce site that will sell royalty-free music, I need an AMAZING product manager who has proven experience in E-Commerce Product design and management. The site already exists and is functional at. However, a ... more

Ecommerce Platform Development | English Proofreading | PHP | Product Management | Search Engine Optimization (SEO) | 5 more

---

Product Manager

Hourly - Entry Level ($) - Est. Time: More than 6 months, 30+ hrs/week - Posted 1 day ago

We are looking for an experienced product manager who will be an integral member of the product development team. You will work alongside our UI designers, front-end and back-end engineers and executives to define, document and articulate the product ... more

---

Lead Continuous Integration / Project Architecture Manager / Lead Dev

Hourly - Expert ($$$) - Est. Time: 3 to 6 months, 30+ hrs/week - Posted 2 days ago

Our company is at the bleeding edge of fintech in the area of Alternative Data in NYC. We provide data services for the top global investment managers, mostly hedge funds. We are looking for an organized and experienced Lead Continuous Integration Project ... more

Agile Project Management | Agile Software Development | Asana | Continuous Integration | Git | 5 more

Examples of product management projects on Upwork

Because the trajectory of a PM is so varied, we don't have a set path we can recommend. The best way to get into this role is to build products in the tech or design capacity with a team, get a variety of experiences under your belt and learn how to become great at building products. We're going to avoid the usual three-month, six-month and one-year timelines for this role as the path varies wildly depending on not only the person you are, but your experiences and the industries you work in. However, here's some courses you can start with to get familiar with the responsibilities of a PM.

Course	Link
Become a Product Manager: Learn the Skills and Get the Job	https://www.udemy.com/become-a-product-manager-learn-the-skills-get-a-job/
The Practitioner's Guide to Product Management by General Assembly	https://www.amazon.com/dp/B00LTUC882/

App and Back-End Development

This Pyjama Category includes Mobile/Desktop/Web App Development and Back-end Development.

Back-end Development, in simple terms means that you will be performing manipulations on data stored in a database. This means reading, writing, creating and updating data using code. While simply understanding how to read and write data on the web should get you started, true back-end code is fairly complex and it might take decades to truly be proficient in a coding language or a framework. The back-end developer creates components and features that are indirectly accessed by a front-end application or system through Application Program Interfaces (APIs)

App development involves writing the front-end applications that the user interacts with. This involves writing an app that works on certain platforms (Android, iOS, Windows, Mac etc), and interfaces with a back-end language to manipulate a database. While each platform has different languages to learn, (iOS has Objective C and Swift, Android has Java, and so on) most developers begin with just one or two. There is also a trend of cross platform technologies like React, React Native and the Ionic Framework that let you write apps once and have them work across all platforms.

The challenge to beginning a career as a back-end developer is to pick a coding language and an associated framework to master. To be a good back-end developer you need to know at least ONE type of ALL of the following skills.

1. Databases—Powered by the language SQL
2. A coding language—this could be C, C#, Ruby, Java, Javascript, Swift
3. A framework—this is a layer (a fancy word to say a set of libraries you can use to make lots of complex functions convenient) built on top of a coding language—C# has ASP.Net, Ruby has Rails, Java has Spring, etc.

While there are several thousand permutations and combinations of databases, coding languages and frameworks, we're going to recommend the simplest and fastest combination which also happens to be one of the most popular combinations online. Simply being able to create an application in Ruby on Rails is enough for you to start billing $30 to 40 an hour—we've seen entry-level freelancers with very little Ruby on Rails experience doing very well for themselves.

To be a good app developer, you need to pick a platform to start with. For beginners, we would recommend ONE of the following:

1. iOS Development, powered by the language Swift
2. Android Development, powered by the language Java
3. Web Development, powered by HTML/CSS and Javascript

With the boom of smartphones, these have the highest demand right now and have ample opportunities to grow. Web app development has been an evergreen skill and will continue to do so with new technologies emerging every couple years.

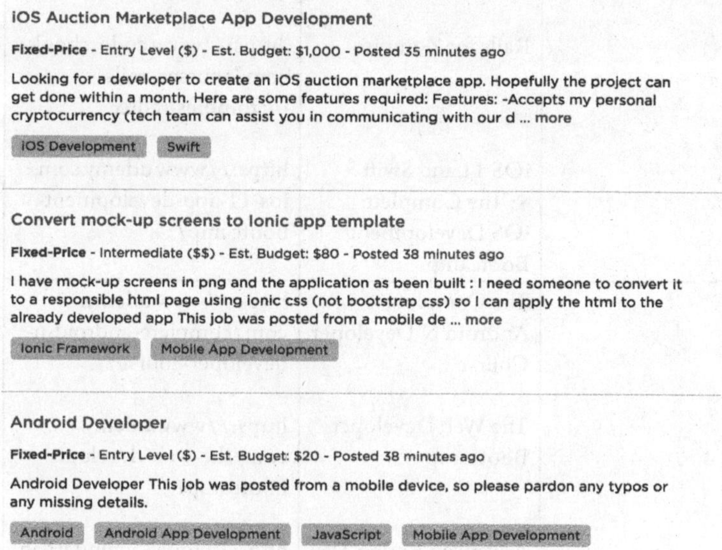

iOS Auction Marketplace App Development

Fixed-Price - Entry Level ($) - Est. Budget: $1,000 - Posted 35 minutes ago

Looking for a developer to create an iOS auction marketplace app. Hopefully the project can get done within a month. Here are some features required: Features: -Accepts my personal cryptocurrency (tech team can assist you in communicating with our d ... more

iOS Development | Swift

Convert mock-up screens to Ionic app template

Fixed-Price - Intermediate ($$) - Est. Budget: $80 - Posted 38 minutes ago

I have mock-up screens in png and the application as been built : I need someone to convert it to a responsible html page using ionic css (not bootstrap css) so I can apply the html to the already developed app This job was posted from a mobile de ... more

Ionic Framework | Mobile App Development

Android Developer

Fixed-Price - Entry Level ($) - Est. Budget: $20 - Posted 38 minutes ago

Android Developer This job was posted from a mobile device, so please pardon any typos or any missing details.

Android | Android App Development | JavaScript | Mobile App Development

Examples of app and back-end development projects on Upwork

Timeline	Name of Course	Link
3 months	HTML and CSS Basics	https://www.codecademy.com/learn/learn-html-css
	Computer Science 101: Master the Theory Behind Programming	https://www.udemy.com/computer-science-101-master-the-theory-behind-programming/
	Ruby Basics Including Object Oriented Programming	https://www.codecademy.com/learn/ruby
Within 6-12 months	Ruby on Rails Course	https://www.codecademy.com/learn/learn-rails
	Rails for Zombies	https://www.codeschool.com/courses/rails-forzombies-redux
	iOS 11 and Swift 4: The Complete iOS Development Bootcamp	https://www.udemy.com/ios-11-app-development-bootcamp/
	The Complete Android N Developer Course	https://www.udemy.com/complete-android-n-developer-course/
	The Web Developer Bootcamp	https://www.udemy.com/the-web-developer-bootcamp/
	Advanced Rails 5 Day Course	http://tutorials.jumpstartlab.com/paths/advanced_rails_five_day.html

Another new field that's been popping up is data science and machine learning, but when it comes to the freelance economy, they're still in the early stages. Most small-to medium-sized business don't need or can't afford machine learning scientists. You are probably better off working full time for a company if you have these skills or want to develop them.

How do I pick?

Now that we've run you through what the best course of action for every Pyjama Category is, it's up to you to pick one that suits your interests. It doesn't matter whether you're a computer programmer who wants to write content or a fashion designer who wants to learn Ruby on Rails. Everything is possible, and we've seen so many people switch streams that we firmly believe your university degree shouldn't limit what you want to learn or the life you want to lead.

So if you've got a useless degree that is making life hard for you, stop using the excuse that you made the wrong choices when you were young and start taking control of the skills you want to have. Learning a skill increases your confidence and makes it easier to learn the next one—we've seen very successful freelancers with a media and communications degree billing $200 an hour as back-end developers and former doctors making a killing doing game design! They all started one step at a time and it was just as daunting for them to let go of their past education and expertise to try their hands at something new. Small victories help you tide over that fear, so get learning!

Creativity

In the midst of picking a skill to learn, mastering the basics, finding a freelance job and making consistent income, creativity is something that can be forgotten. Learning any of the skills we've talked about doesn't guarantee that you'll be creative.

It's like teaching someone the piano—you may know all of the keystrokes and can play songs from memory or by looking at sheet music, but creativity lies in being able to use the keystrokes in a new and original way that sounds good when played. Similarly, *learning* how to design a website, writing content or designing a game is all about teaching yourself fundamental techniques, limitations, possibilities and how to make whatever you are able to see.

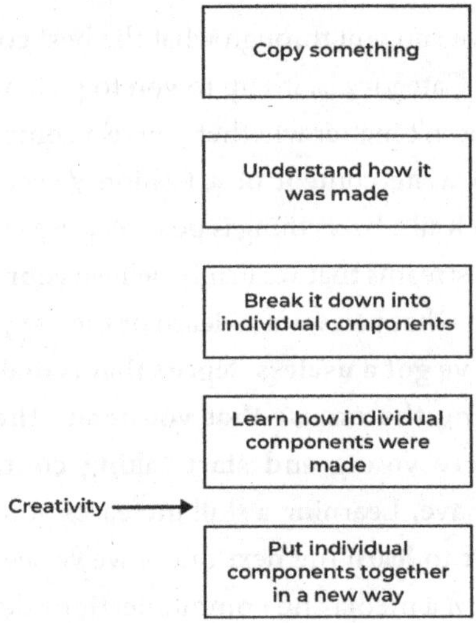

Where creativity plays into the equation of freelance work

Creativity lies in being able to use those individual skills in a manner that results in something truly original that looks and functions well. We cannot account for how long it will take you to develop creativity or how that will help you better your income, so throughout this book we're going to sidestep the topic of creativity and focus on more objective matters.

Passion vs Money

It seems fairly shallow for us to consistently bring up things like billing rate, income and how much money you're going to make. It seems like we're being completely dispassionate about the projects we're working on. I personally believe that passion is an overused word. Why is it so difficult for us as human beings to say we want to learn something to make money? A lot of the decisions we make in our waking life are somehow related to money; so why the secrecy when it comes to being able to have financially enriched lives?

Having a consistent income can enable you to explore further and find what really drives you. Money is what that gives me the freedom to pursue my real passions. If I don't have to spend 10 hours a day working, I can devote that time to the things I care about—building cool things, learning music, playing and making video games, spending time with my friends and family and anything else I might want to do.

So get rid of the misconception that you need to be passionate to learn a skill that makes you money—just go ahead and learn it, then see how that skill becomes your ability to earn your freedom to do the things that drive you. Nobody is born with a passion for something; it's something that you have to constantly discover in life. A friend of mine who's a top accountant in the country once said to me that he wasn't born with the passion to balance books, but once he got really good at it, he discovered that it was something he enjoyed doing.

So forget passion for now.

The only thing that really works is **discipline**. Be disciplined about learning. Get over the initial learning curve of a skill, and get good at it. Get over the learning curves of multiple skills if you aren't able to decide what's best for you. I can guarantee that once you start to enjoy the process and being in a flow state, a passion for it will develop inside you.

In my case, I absolutely hated learning to build a website or an app. The process was frustrating and took me longer than most people who actually liked to code. The trade-off was that it gave me the ability to build absolutely anything I dreamt of online, something I can't do without today. I'm passionate about building awesome things. I'm not passionate about writing codes. However, codes allow me to build the things I'm passionate about. So I decided to go ahead and learn it.

Chapter 4

Communicating Your Value

"You don't get paid for the hour. You get paid for the value you bring to the hour."

—Jim Rohn

Why is value communication important?

Every freelance gig has many bidders—whether somebody referred you to a business in real life, or you applied to a project online. For a business to hire you, they have to be convinced that you're the perfect person for the job and hiring you will give them better returns than hiring anyone else.

So how do you win? The answer is plain and simple—communication. You might be the best person for a job, and have all the experience and skills to make it a success, but unless you find a way to make your client believe that, you're not going to win.

Every single touchpoint between you and the client is communication. Whether it's pitching your services over Skype or them going through your online profile—they form an impression of you and this influences their decision.

How much should I charge?

Every client is different. The industry they're in, the size of their business, the urgency of their need, their past experiences with freelancers and many more factors play an influence. But before we get into that, let's understand the two basic types of billing that you can work with: Fixed price and hourly. We'll also talk about a hybrid model we've seen freelancers adopting.

Fixed Price

A fixed price project is one where the price of the project is mutually agreed upon before work begins. For example, say a client wants you to build a social networking app and you mutually agree to a budget of $500 for three discussed features. The scope here is static.

Typically, you get paid in milestones. After you complete your first feature and demo it, 1/3rd of the fixed price will be wired to you, after the next feature, another 1/3rd and the full amount after the final feature has been built and demonstrated. As a sign of commitment from both sides, it is also recommended to take an upfront payment of anywhere between 10–40% of the project cost.

Some fixed price projects might pay you only at the end when the final product is demonstrated. Stay away from such projects because there's a high chance that the client will disappear after the final email or that the end will never be reached as new changes and edits are continuously requested. This, of course, can happen when there are milestones too, but they help reduce the risk for both the freelancer and the client.

Hourly

An hourly billing project is one where you get paid for every hour of work you put in. Your hourly rate is decided beforehand, a rough budget is agreed upon, you track your time whenever you work and send the timesheets along with your invoice. The scope here is dynamic.

Platforms like Upwork usually require you to install a time tracking software that monitors your work. They track keystroke activity and take a screenshot of your work every 10 minutes to make sure you're not billing the client for idle hours or reporting more hours than you've actually worked.

Outside of platforms, the hourly system works only on trust. A client will trust that you will get your work done in the time it requires, and you trust that the client will pay you for this time.

Hybrid (Weekly Billing)

A model that some freelancers in my network have been using is a hybrid model of weekly billing. You sell the client chunks of your time, one week at a time. So, for example, if you expect a project to take about a hundred hours but it could possibly be more depending on changes and edits, then you can give them a fixed cost per week, with additional weeks if things stretch.

The advantage of this hybrid model is that clients that are hesitant about hourly billing can find some solace in the fixed prices of this model. Another advantage is that if the project stretches beyond your initial estimate, you can always sell them additional weeks to get the work done. It is then in the client's best interest to provide timely feedback and wrap up the project with little delay.

Start billing at a price you're comfortable with and clients are willing to pay. After you have a few reviews and ratings, increase your billing rate dynamically. Avoid working fixed price in the beginning as you probably have a poor understanding of how long it will take to finish a project. Also, fixed price clients at lower price ranges are very finicky and keep demanding changes. Remember that you're eventually going to wean off whatever platform you're using and work with your own clients. Most of the SIZR crew stayed on Upwork for less than a year before moving on to private projects.

Value-Based Pricing

What might be affordable and hold great value for client one might be too expensive and unaffordable for client two, and might be suspiciously low and hold questionable value to client three. The magic is in finding the balance—a sweet spot that is the perfect intersection of the client's expectations and your skills.

When I started out, I saw job posts with 50 to 100 applicants. For a beginner, this can be intimidating and I started by bidding very low. I bid $3 an hour on my first few applications and landed zero jobs. For high value clients, my skills weren't up to the mark. For low value clients, I was suspiciously cheap. Most of them actually have a subconscious range—they know they want cheap but too cheap raises suspicions about your quality. So I slowly started bidding higher, until I found my sweet spot—$10 an hour. For the first few months, I did all my projects at $10 an hour. As I worked up, I got the confidence to bill $20, then $40 and so on. My value was what I chose to make it, as long as I could communicate and deliver, I could charge anything! So one day I did something risky—I left Upwork and started freelancing by myself.

I took up a project that I got via a referral. A client I was billing $40 an hour ran a start-up in San Francisco and referred me to his friend in a very big Silicon Valley company. They had a marketing event coming up and needed a landing page to promote the event and collect registrations. This was my first project off a platform and I was a little concerned. There were a couple of questions in my mind, namely:

1. ***What if this client doesn't pay?*** Most projects on platforms are covered by some kind of guarantee for both sides. They do what they can to make sure neither the client nor the freelancer gets scammed.
2. ***Was I really capable of working for a Fortune 500 company?*** This was a world away from the small business I'd been working with so far. What could someone like me possibly offer them?

To add to my confusion, my college exams were the following week. Everybody around me was in crunch mode, spending late nights huddled over books.

With all these things in mind, I had a sudden moment of clarity. I was going to do this project. I had been presented with an opportunity that I just couldn't miss. I added the client's friend on Skype and we had a talk.

After a quick discussion, we decided that I would bill them $100 an hour. We signed a bunch of paperwork, including non-disclosure agreements and work contracts (this was new to me, since Upwork usually handles all of this). They would pay me via PayPal for the hours I'd logged and required me to be "on call" four days a week at a very particular time.

It was new and exciting, but also intimidating. I went ahead and did it anyway.

In two weeks, I had accrued $7,000 working little over five hours a day. I was 20 years old at that time and in my second year of college but I'd managed to figure something out that was hidden in plain sight from me all along.

Impressed with my work, the company's product head referred me to another client with pay in the same ballpark and then more followed. I worked with clients in their network for the next six months, getting better at my core skill but also the skill of communication. Most of that money went on to fuel Jobspire's first year of operations before we raised early stage VC money. In the two years since then, the skills I learnt have carried over to every project I've worked on.

Chapter 5

The Platform Game

"Waves are the practise of water."

—SHUNRYU SUZUKI

If you've picked one of the Pyjama Categories and completed your first milestone somewhere in the one to three month window, then congratulations! Now, while learning is continuous and you have a long way to go, you're ready to play the Platform Game.

Where do I land my first project?

Before I talk about the Platform Game, I'd like to give you a tour of the most viable platforms to start freelancing on. Remember, your goal is to one day reach a point where more people want to work with you than you have the time for. That is, purely off referrals from your previous clients. Working on freelance platforms is a means to that end.

There's a new freelance platform launched every couple of months. We put platforms into one of two categories—**horizontal** platforms or **vertical** platforms.

Horizontal Platforms

These are general purpose freelancing platforms with all kinds of clients, posting all kinds of projects, across different industries and skills. No matter which of the Pyjama Categories you end up picking, you will be able to create a profile on these and start bidding for projects that suit you. Some examples of these are Upwork and Freelancer. We would highly recommend Upwork (formed after a merger of Odesk and Elance) as it's the one we got our start on, and is the biggest platform in the world. They normally charge a percentage of the total project cost as a fee and have protections and limitations in place to ensure both sides have a positive experience.

Vertical Platforms

There are a couple of differential factors between horizontal and vertical platforms. This factor can be the type of projects they work with—a platform for freelance content writing, a platform for graphic design, a platform for marketers etc. The factor could also be the scale of projects, and hence the budget—a platform for solo business owners to find freelancers, a platform for small- and medium-sized business to find freelancers, a platform for the world's top companies to find the best freelancers. Some examples are TopTal, Gigster, Crew, ContentMart, etc.

The Platform Game

I call it the Platform Game because most freelancers start their freelance careers on platforms like Upwork before either moving completely to off-platform referrals, or finding their balance of platform and off-platform projects. Think of platforms as your training ground for freelancing and also your first source of projects. You'll have more sources later but to start with, they're the sole source.

Now, when I call it a game, I'm in no way devaluing the importance of these platforms or the seriousness of work. I'm simply helping you recognize that there are other players and it's a competitive landscape. You have to work hard, put in the time and do your best to get a favourable outcome for your clients and yourself. You will be rewarded for your efforts in due time, but it can be easy to get disillusioned after sending 50 proposals and not getting a single reply. Everybody goes through that and the key is to keep playing the game without giving up. Be the best player you can to the best of your capacity and eventually the game will recognize it and reward you when the time is right.

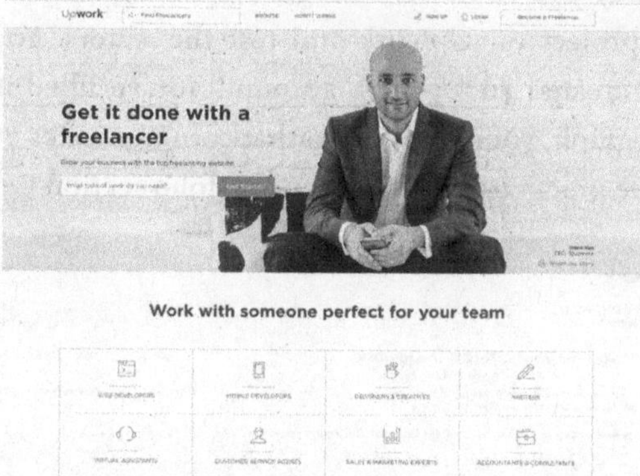

Upwork is one of the most popular freelancing platforms right now

Platforms help you find projects, send proposals, track milestones and billing, manage communication and get paid with a guarantee. They even maintain a profile for you which contains samples of your work, testimonials on past projects and hourly rate which helps clients make better decisions. The only caveat is that there's a lot of competition, with each project receiving 5 to 10 bids at the very least, and 50 to 100 bids at the most.

Platforms are like a training ground where you get paid to get better at your skills.

When you're confident in your skills and are familiar with the ins and outs of freelancing, you can branch out and get projects outside of platforms. When you reach this level, you have to take care of sourcing, sending proposals, contracts, tracking milestones and so on. This can be hard for someone who's just starting out with a small portfolio of work, so go this route when you feel like you're ready.

Your Player Profile

So, you think you've learnt enough of one Pyjama Category to take up a project on Upwork and test the waters. You've gone ahead and created an Upwork account. You've filled it up with your photograph, your skills, a bio that communicates your value, maybe some practice projects in the portfolio section.

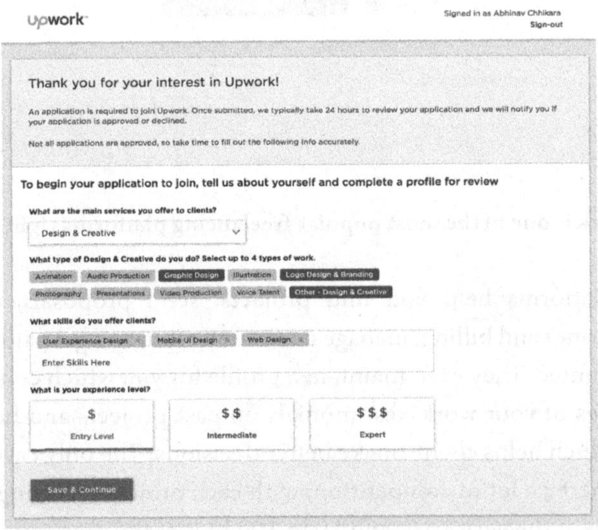

Setting up a profile on Upwork

Now comes the time to apply (also called bidding) to projects. You bid on a few, but receive no responses!

To get a job in one of the Pyjama Categories, you absolutely need to have a portfolio of work. This helps clients figure out if you actually have the skills you claim and it can be a differentiator when picking between multiple proposals.

But wait! You haven't done any projects yet; how are you supposed to have a portfolio?

This is a bit of a catch-22 situation. You need projects to build your portfolio, but you also need a portfolio to get projects.

The best approach to this problem is the one mentioned in chapter two—it was to apply for as many projects as possible, bid super low and somehow manage to get a project in any possible way. This might take some time and you'll have to apply for as many projects as you can since your profile is new to Upwork and has zero projects. To a client, you're a risky bet because your profile has no testimonials or work history. Keep at it and you'll eventually get a project. After all, everyone is in this position at the start of their journey and must overcome it.

Your Superpowers

If you've been following our learning plan, you've taken your skill from zero to something. You're now better than the average person when it comes to that skill and that's something people will pay you for.

Consider this: You've picked graphic design and you're now capable of creating decent looking posters in Photoshop. You're ready for your first project and making some money from this skill but you don't know how to proceed.

Meanwhile, on the other side of the world, Nate is a movie theater owner in Memphis, Tennessee. He's looking to increase the number of walk-ins his establishment gets from the shopping district nearby. He has zero skills in designing flyers and could really use some help.

Put yourself in Nate's shoes for a minute.

His idea is to print one thousand flyers next week with the current movie they're running and have someone distribute them in the street. Each movie ticket is priced at $7. If he can get his establishment out in front of one thousand people, that's $7,000 of potential business and that's just for one week.

To Nate, the value of someone designing really good looking flyers is a couple thousand dollars in revenue.

Bidding and Proposals

There are hundreds of listings like these on Upwork and each of them gets tens of applicants daily. The easier the skill; the greater the number of applicants. But here's a trick that will make you stand out: Most of these applicants follow what we call the 'water hose' strategy of applying to jobs. They know that if they apply to a hundred jobs, most likely a couple of those will convert. So they apply a generic template and spray it everywhere.

This is what Nate receives in his inbox:

> *Respected Sir/Ma'am, we're a graphic design, SEO/SMM and digital marketing agency who give our 110% to make sure all our client needs are met. We have a top full-time team who will take care of your every need. We were established in 2007 and since then we have done over 800 projects ... (Links to 60 websites)*

Not just one, but 20 variations of this same template. If you don't believe me and want to see this for yourself, put yourself in a client's position and try posting a project on Upwork for your category. You'll very quickly see that the responses that stand out to you will be the ones that are highly personalized, have high success rates according to their profiles, and don't look like spam.

While writing proposals, think about whether you're talking about yourself or talking about the value your skills can bring. The water hose strategy probably works for some people but personalization and thoughtfulness will make you stand out in the crowd. When you try to understand the client's perspective and the problem they have, you can position your skills as a solution and talk about how you're going to deliver on it.

What Nate needs right now is someone who can say:

> *"Hey Nate, I had read through your job description and it sounds like something I can help you with! I've had experience in designing flyers in the past for local restaurants and I've received great feedback from them. I am attaching a couple of samples for you to have a look.*
>
> *I should be able to complete your work within a week. Would love to have a Skype call to discuss further, here are my details!"*

You've taken the time to read the requirements of the job, you've **personalized** your cover letter to **highlight the skills** needed and why you're a perfect fit, and you've mentioned a **timeline for successful completion** of the project. Feel free to get creative in your cover letter but include these basics to make sure you're making the right impression.

Let's recap:

1. Personalize your cover letter.
2. Highlight your skills.
3. Mention a timeline for successful completion of your project.

Making a Charismatic Bid

While you have a fair chance of landing a project simply by following the three steps above, let's go ahead and add some humour and personality to your bid. It's up to you to find your personal balance of personality and professionalism and find out what works best to convert a lead into a successful project. Here's a sample:

> *Hey Nate! I had a read through your job description and it sounds like something I can help you out with! I've had experience in designing flyers in the past for local restaurants and I've received great feedback from them. I am attaching a couple of samples for you to have a look.*
>
> *You can check out some of my other work at: www.yourpersonalwebsite.com*
>
> *Apart from my great photoshop skills, I'm also a stand-up comedian on weekends. Prepare for your Skype calls with me to be a ton of fun!*
>
> *Ciao.*

As you can see, mentioning that you're a stand-up comedian, or a musician or whatever adds flavour and passion to your cover letter makes it easier for you to stand out. Not just that, it becomes easier to negotiate and justify a higher billing rate because most clients pay a small premium to work with fun people!

Game Rewards

If you play the game honestly, delivering the maximum value to clients and patiently levelling up, you will be rewarded. Not only will the rate for your services skyrocket, but so will social capital like testimonials, five star ratings, repeat projects and referrals.

The prices for services in the Pyjama Categories vary a lot based on the type of client and the scope of the project, among other things. To start, pick a minimum price you're okay with. Be honest with yourself and don't spend too much time coming up with this initial number. You can always change this for every project you apply to.

On most horizontal platforms, the proposals for projects vary from $3 an hour, up to the hundreds. So try not to worry about your competition but try to pitch your value clearly in the cover letter and justify the amount you're charging. With one or two projects under your belt, you'll have a better idea of what your market rate is.

Communication is Key

One of the biggest problems clients face with freelancers is that of communication. If you're sitting in Bengaluru with a client in Portland, not only do you have a massive time difference, but also zero visibility. Contrast this with a full-time job in Bengaluru, where all your colleagues show up at 10AM and leave at 7PM, you can easily walk up to anyone and see what they're working on and you have visibility into what everyone is up to.

You're working remotely in freelance jobs. "Remote" is a term used to denote that you're not working in the same office as someone else. You're getting the benefits of flexibility, improved purchasing power and freedom, but you've got to earn it. You have to make the client feel as comfortable working with you as they would with someone working in their office.

Imagine this scenario: You have a Skype call with Nate, and he's excited to work with you. He awards you the contract and gives you the description of what he wants the first two flyers to be like. You're ready to get started.

Day 1: You sketch out some ideas for what they could look like.

Day 2: You start designing some early versions in Photoshop.

Day 3: You continue refining the ideas in Photoshop.

Day 4: You've reached a stage where the flyers look pretty good.

This is what that looks like to Nate:

Day 1: I'm excited! Hope this turns out well.

Day 2: I wonder how it's going.

Day 3: What's happening?

Day 4: Oh god, what if I've been scammed.

See what happened here? There are two things to keep in mind: **Managing expectations and consistent communication.**

After you've discussed the terms and what the client wants, set expectations early. What is your process normally like? How long does each part of your process take? When will you have the first update ready? When can you get on a call next?

Being transparent with your style of working and your process keeps clients happy. Let's say this is what you send:

> *Hey Nate, excited to get started! The call really helped understand what you need from me.*
>
> *Here's what you can expect in terms of how I work and rough timelines: I usually take a day or two to sketch out ideas and get started with the initial concept design. Once I've done this, I'll be sending over an email with some options, so we can pick which direction to go in. Once we've established that, I'll spend about the next three days refining the flyers and getting them ready for print. By the end of the week, we should be ready for a test run!*

This establishes what the typical timeline for the project looks like, when the client should expect to hear from you next and what successful completion within deadlines will look like. This removes anxiety on the client's side and establishes you as a professional who's not going to get flaky and abandon the project.

This is what it now looks like at Nate's end:

Day 1: I'm excited!

Day 2: Will wait for an update tomorrow.

Day 3: *receives email from you*

Day 4: Will wait for the next update.

Day 5: *receives final design and asks for an edit*

Day 6: Completed and ready to go!

When do you stop playing?

You can play it for as long as you want. Platforms are great training grounds when you start, but when you get good at it, two things happen. First, you get to a point when the game becomes easier; you get projects every couple of months and have a good inbound stream of income. You can stay at this level for however long you'd like, but whenever you feel like moving to something bigger, start keeping an eye out. Platforms are only one source of projects but there are many other sources out there.

There's a whole world of businesses out there that have never heard of Upwork and could use your services. It's up to you how you discover them and pitch your value. These are *outbound* proposals. In the next few chapters, we'll talk about how you can increase outbound proposals with cold emails, as well as inbound leads by establishing an online presence, or a personal brand.

Learning to write proposals and managing client expectation is a skill and you're going to get better over time. As you get better at your skill, your process will improve and you'll understand your working style better. You'll also understand how to best deal with clients and how to avoid disaster.

Repeat Projects and Referrals

This is the #1 source of new projects if you play your cards right and successfully deliver on your promise. If you're delivering value to existing clients and creating outstanding work, they'll be more than happy to refer you to their friends and other business owners. Repeat projects and referrals will drive a huge chunk of your projects in the future, so try to keep your clients happy and go the extra mile. On the successful completion of a project, feel free to directly ask them for feedback on your work, about similar future projects, and whether they'd be willing to make referrals.

Personal Connections

Do you know someone in your own network who could use your help? This could be a family member or a friend who owns a business and needs your help. Or, it could even be local businesses near you. Depending upon the people you know and the country you live in, you could have varied success at this. Personally in India, I had no success with this during the first four years of freelancing. But, as the demand for my skills caught up in India and I grew my network, this started to increase until it made up more than 90% of my projects.

Online Directories

Try to visualize what your ideal client looks like and think about where you can find them online. If you're a content writer for start-ups, try looking at ProductHunt or other start-up directories where you can find potential clients. If you're a 3D modeller, hang out in game development forums online and have conversations with people there. If you're a marketer who's worked on running ads for local businesses, look up Craigslist and see if there's anyone looking for what you offer. Get creative.

When things go bad

As you work on more projects, you'll understand what kind of clients you like working with and the kind you don't. Some clients will be a delight to work with and some clients will be a pain. That's totally normal. The clients that might be a delight to work with for some freelancers might be a pain to others. It's about finding and working with people who enable you to produce your best work.

There are particular types of clients that you will enjoy working with and types you will want to keep away from. The only way you can find out is by working on all kinds of projects till it becomes obvious to you. Observe your working relationship, the way it makes you feel, the things that are important to you and the things that irk you.

Saying No

Initially, you might feel like saying YES to all projects that come your way to build your portfolio, and that's great! Over time, you'll start figuring out what good clients look like and the red flags that mean a bad client. Also, remember that your goal should be to one day stop using a freelancing platform and be able to land clients on your own. To do that, you need to create an awesome portfolio. You cannot have an awesome portfolio with 200 flyers for different small businesses. Pick clients that will give you opportunities to showcase your skills on bigger and better platforms. A $5 an hour project from Google is better than a $100 project from an unknown client. Why? Because simply having Google on your portfolio will help you land massive projects. No client needs to know how much you billed the previous client.

Firing Clients

After working on a project, you might start to realize that you hate working on it. This might be because of the client's style of working or it could be because of the nature of work, or anything else. Projects like these drain your productivity and you'll most likely end up procrastinating.

Have a talk with your client and very clearly tell them what's going on. It could be that it simply isn't working out for you or that you have other commitments that are preventing you from completing the project. The earlier you clarify, the better it is. The client might have deadlines that they need to hit, and they can start looking for other freelancers. You can even make a referral if possible, making the transition easy for them.

Community

Find other people like you and talk to them. There are online communities, subreddits and Facebook groups you can join where you can ask questions if you ever feel stuck. The situation you're facing is probably not unique and someone has probably faced something similar before. Reading about how other freelancers work and their processes helps you understand your skills from a professional's perspective and helps you in refining your own process. So, read and research as much as you can!

Chapter 6
The Freelancer's Mindset

> *"People with goals succeed because they know where they're going."*
>
> —Earl Nightingale

Setting targets

How do you know how well you're playing, if you haven't set targets? Targets help you make sense of your progress and help you move forward and discover what your bigger goals are.

Tangible vs Ambiguous

Let's take an example to understand how to effectively set targets and what makes something tangible or ambiguous. If you're in your early to mid-20s, your targets probably sound like this:

- Travel the world.
- Make enough money to not worry about food and shelter.
- Save up for a car.

While these might be alright, there's no tangibility here. If you really wanted to travel the world, you would eventually end up doing it when the time was right. But when it comes to holding yourself accountable, it helps to set **tangible targets and goals, with realistic timelines and numbers.**

This is the only way to get things done and avoid distraction and confusion caused by abstract targets. Don't get me wrong; big targets are perfectly fine. But unless you attach tangibility to them, you will be disappointed every now and then because you will constantly feel like you're not achieving anything. Looking at the same targets above, here's how some of the smartest people I know would frame them:

- Travel to Paris and see the Mona Lisa within the next four years.
- Make at least ₹ 3,000 a day within the next four years.
- Save ₹ 8,000 for every month in a fixed deposit at 6% return in order to afford a hatchback within four years.

This way of thinking might make life sound extremely mechanical. But when you set clear, tangible, achievable targets, it sets you up for a life with less stress. There's still plenty of room for spontaneity! The biggest cause of stress is ambiguity—not feeling in control of your life and worrying about things you have little or no control over.

Coming back to freelance, setting targets will not just help you learn and grow but also help you stay motivated. While everyone should have their own targets—these are the targets we think are achievable in three months, six months, one year and two years.

Freelancing Targets

Within 3 months	Learn your core skill and land your first project
Within 6 months	Land upto 4 supplementary skills and touch $25 in hourly billing

Within 1 year	Consistently bill $40 hourly and have a pipeline of steady projects for 3 months
Within 2 years	Reach the upper limits of your industry's billing rate, have a 3 month consistent project pipeline and start building side projects and passive income

Surprisingly, everyone at SIZR followed this timeline independently. While we did make our share of mistakes, it was remarkable how, at any given time, we were all on the same trajectory and learnt similar things. I think this is a very good timeline to have and **if you have a full-time job, the six-month to one-year mark is probably when you can think about quitting.**

Common questions

What is the Ceiling? How Much Money Can I Make if I Get Really Good at This Freelance Game?

While Forbes predicts that half of the American workforce will be freelancers by 2020, the question is how many freelancers will make top dollar. We know freelancers who work exclusively on platforms and make over $200k a year. There are freelancers who work in their own networks who make millions of dollars a year. Of course, there's a category even beyond—some making 8 figures a year. Most of these people also end up diversifying, using their skills to build side projects, selling merchandise, software and tools, building small businesses and more. In fact, at that level you would become more of an entrepreneur than a freelancer.

At SIZR, we used to do similar things—we built small tools and software for business on the side. We had already started building Jobspire at some point and we were selling stuff on an e-commerce platform we had built—a smooth, diversified flow of money that continued to bring us returns even if all us decided to go away on vacation for a month or two.

The Full-Time Freelancer vs the Pocket Money Freelancer

So far, all our discussion has been focused on how freelancing replaces your primary income. There's also the possibility that you could use your skills to make supplementary income. This is also perfectly legal as long as you are not stealing clients from your company or working on something that directly competes with what your company does. The pocket money freelancer is a hybrid, someone who devotes a small amount of time to freelancing. Most of us started out as pocket money freelancers until we gained the confidence and the portfolio to do it full time.

The biggest problem with being a pocket money freelancer, however great your skills are, is the shortage of quality projects. Most business owners who are serious about projects would prefer to hire full-time freelancers rather than extending deadlines for part-timers. However, shorter 2–4 week jobs are great to make supplementary income. It's best to use a freelance platform as your primary source in such cases and explore additional sources when you feel ready for it.

Why Should I Freelance When I Can Get a Stable Salary?

The answer to this question depends on where you live. If you're an Indian like me, freelancing is a no-brainer and you can easily expect to make 3–10 times more than your current salary assuming you are an average 20–25 year old. In the United States, the "job for life" may be a thing of the past for most people, but at least for the next five years, salaried employment is more secure than freelancing. You get a regular pay cheque, and as long as you do a good job, you can rely on that pay cheque each month. Even if you get fired, your employer will usually have to give you some notice or provide some compensation. Not to mention perks like insurance and other benefits.

However, in India that situation changes. The average IT software professional at the beginning of their career might make between ₹ 3 lakh and ₹ 5 lakh a year. Non-IT roles make even less.

Let's do some quick math to show you why freelancing in India makes sense:

At 52 workweeks of 40 hours each, there are 2,080 working hours per year. If you subtract vacation time, sick leave and public holidays from this, it comes up to around 1,800 hours per year.

Now, remember that you're not going to spend all your time freelancing—you might spend some time applying to projects, sending invoices, marketing, paperwork, etc. Let's assume that it takes up 25% of your time, which means out of 1,800 you have 1,350 hours available.

From a billing rate perspective, let's consider a goal of $40 an hour with a steady stream of projects. Multiplying your hourly rate by 1,350, you should be making $54,000 a year which translates into roughly ₹ **3,500,000,** which is almost 10 times what the average salaried IT professional makes in India.

Making $54,000 a year would be considered *lower middle class* in America, but since you're competing on a level playing field, *the internet,* you can make the same kind of money sitting at home in India. Of course, as you fine-tune your craft, you can start making even more per hour, and at $100 an hour billing rate—standard for a good back-end developer, you could be making $135,000, which is a whopping ₹ **8,778,000** per year.

In the United States, $135,000 would put you in the *upper middle-class* category but in India that kind of income would allow you to easily retire within a decade. At its peak, SIZR was billing

$100-$150 an hour, but what we found at that point is that instead of selling services, we could sell products to developed countries, effectively reducing the total amount of effort we put in and have a passive stream of income rivaling what freelancing brought us!

Will I be Good Enough to Make $40 an Hour? How Long Will It Take?

Assuming you have good communication skills, you pick a Pyjama Category, other than data entry, and are prepared to make certain commitments, $40 an hour is a very achievable target **within one year**. I may sound like a broken record, but $40 an hour is a middle-class income range in America and you're competing on a level playing field. However, to succeed, you need to commit to a few things:

1. You follow our approach to tangible goal setting and set clear three month, six month and one year goals.
2. You follow high quality learning material and work on your skills.
3. You develop a passion for building things and learning how technology works.
4. You follow our advice on bidding and building a personal brand.
5. You build a network of likeminded friends and keep yourself motivated, but more importantly, disciplined.

Before we go ahead, I want to tell you a story about one of Jobspire's first interns—Yash. Yash was a bright young kid who came to us in his second year of college for an internship. At that point, he wanted to get into a company like Google real bad and was hoping that we teach him enough so he could apply to a bigger company. What happened over the next few months surprised him but not the Jobspire team.

Despite being an intern at Jobspire, I recommended that he learn how to build a website and freelance by himself. One thing I notice a lot of the times when I recommend people to freelance is the apprehension. The uncertainty and the thought that is always at the back of their minds is that this might not work out because nobody around them has done it or has succeeded at doing it. What I did at that point was to open my browser and place in front of his eyes my entire PayPal history. **The easiest way to convince a human being is not argument but proof.**

Yash decided to give it a shot, taught himself how to build a website in a month and bagged his first project in his second month interning with us. It was a $6 an hour project, but it wasn't the money that changed Yash. He had proved to himself that this worked, and *that is the most powerful thing you can do for yourself.* In the SIZR circle, we call it the **First Project Effect** and simply landing and completing your first project will give you such a different perspective of economy and time as money, that you end up planning the rest your life completely differently! The most fearless entrepreneurs I know went through some variation of the First Project effect—whether it be building a website or selling raffle tickets.

Today, Yash runs his own start-up, and regardless of whether it succeeds or fails, I'm proud to be one of his mentors. Both of us know what brought him here—his first project! The point I'm trying to make here is simple—if freelancing scares you, **successfully land and complete one project.** Trust me, *everything will change.*

Chapter 7
Your Personal Brand

"All of us need to understand the importance of branding. We are CEOs of our own companies: Me, Inc. To be in business today, our most important job is to be head marketer for the brand called you."

—Tom Peters

Once you're a couple projects in and have spent some time freelancing, your next goal is to get a consistent pipeline of projects to keep you going. One way to do this is to focus on the number of inbound queries you receive and reduce your reliance on outbound proposals. This saves you the time you'd normally spend on finding leads and bidding for projects.

That sounds great in theory, but how do you reach a level where you receive a couple enquiries every week?

Authority

Consider this situation: Melissa runs a health blog for millennials to get started with dieting and healthy eating. She normally publishes two articles a week and has seen a huge uptick in the number of visitors over the past three months. She wants to take it to the next level and get a freelancer onboard to help her with article research and content.

She posts a job on Upwork and also asks her network for recommendations for a content writer. She gets about 30 proposals on Upwork and a couple of recommendations from friends and other bloggers. She narrows it down to two candidates:

The first is Arun; an applicant on Upwork. He has a good profile, decent work history and a portfolio of articles he's written for his clients in the past.

The second is Kyle, a freelancer recommended by her friend. He runs a blog with resources to help other blog owners write better content and build better relationships with their readers. Melissa goes through his blog and finds great suggestions on how she can scale her own blog. He's also written an e-book on managing your blog's content publishing calendar which she immediately downloads and reads.

Which do you think sounds like the better bet? In most cases, the choice is pretty obvious. Arun might be good at content marketing, but Kyle has literally written a *book* on content marketing. Although, it involved no extra work other than maintaining his blog, his work has already delivered tremendous value to Melissa for free. He's established himself as an expert and an authority on the subject.

First steps

As you've guessed by now, the way to get inbound leads is to establish **yourself as an authority in your core skill.** This sounds scary and super difficult. After all, you might have started learning your core skills only a couple of months back!

There are two things you need to do to establish yourself as an authority:

1. Be better than the average person in your skill.
2. Share what you know and teach others.

An excellent book on this topic is *Authority* by Nathan Barry. One of the core ideas of the book is that people who you regard as 'experts' in your field are **simply people who've bothered to share their work and teach others.** Try to think about people you consider experts in their field, and you'll realize that it's because they put out content related to their skill and that's how you've heard about them in the first place.

Personal brand

To most people, the definition of a personal brand is a **website and a logo** for their freelance business. They're definitely two of the components of a personal brand, but consider this—if no one ever sees your site, does it even exist?

Remember the following things:

To make your brand valuable, you need to put out content.

To make your content seen, you need to drive traffic to it.

To drive traffic to your content, it has to be useful.

To be useful content, it has to teach people something they don't know or offer a unique perspective.

What, Where and How

The What, Where, and How of establishing yourself as an authority are the key to getting more leads and therefore, new clients.

What Do I Create?

Content comes in many forms. It could be blog posts, videos, infographics, e-books, resources, etc. Teach what you know. Your perspective while just starting out is very different from the perspective of people who've been working on it for years. Back in the day people only listened to experts. Today, people want to listen to those who have just started out, people who have an intermediate level of skill and people who are "almost there", so they can plan their own roadmap.

This is where the concept of authority comes in. Think about your field, and who you consider to be the experts in it. It's the people creating great stuff and putting it out there. It's the ones who care about their craft and like talking about it online. They're usually not the ones who're working in isolation and keeping it to themselves. In the age of the internet, you might be great at what you do, but unless you put it out there and help others, your presence and impact is nil.

When you create and share content related to your field, it serves a dual purpose. Other freelancers in your field come across your content, possibly learn something from it and are grateful. The next time someone asks them how to do something, they'd rather link to your guide than explain it themselves. I've done this multiple times myself, when I'd rather link to a friend's blog post or tutorial rather than teach something from scratch. This sows the seeds of establishing yourself as an expert.

The other purpose this achieves is that it gives potential clients an entry point to understanding your process, how you work and your skill. By reading what you've written, it helps them understand how you approach your work and helps them relate your experiences to their own problems. So before they even reach out to you, you've earned their trust.

But What if I'm Not Good Enough?

This is the number one reason that stops people from sharing more online. I get it; it's scary making something and putting it out there when you know for a fact that there's so many people better than you. It stopped me from sharing too, I wanted to wait till I got "good enough" before I started to share.

Over time, what I realized was that you'll never think you're good enough because there will always be someone better than you. Someone who works much harder, someone who is a lot more skilled than you are, someone with years of experience on you and someone with big brands in their portfolio.

On the flipside, there's always someone who's just started and is looking for guidance. Someone who would get started if they only knew where to begin. Someone who's worked on lesser projects than you have, someone who's not put in as much time as you have.

Document your learning process in public. The way I started sharing more designs online and more articles about my work was by treating it as a process of documentation, but in public. With fast-paced changes in technology, there's always a new or better way to do things that established experts in the field might not have considered. There's innovation happening at the fringes, and by documenting publically, you're making yourself a part of the tech adoption curve and bringing in awareness.

The selfish reason to put out content is simply that teaching and writing are the best ways to understand something. It forces you to distil abstract concepts into insights and explain it in simple words. Investing in your future this way will contribute to more inbound inquiries.

Where is This Content Hosted?

What's just as important as creating content is where you'll be putting it. I mentioned something similar earlier, and it applies here too: if you create content and nobody consumes it, does it even exist?

If you're creating blog posts, you could create a Wordpress site for hosting it or you could post them on Medium.com.

If you're creating videos, you could post them on YouTube or Vimeo.

If you're creating graphics, you could post them on Pinterest, on your blog, or on graphic design specific sites like Behance or Dribbble.

Experiment with where you host your content and how it affects traffic. For example—if you create a blog on Wordpress, nobody will read it unless you drive traffic to it. On the other hand, if your blog is on Medium, it will be seen by their users, thanks to their inbuilt distribution.

Our approach to this was simple—we built websites for ourselves but also experimented with external platforms. You can check out abhinavc.com or varunmayya.com to see our public websites. Most of our inbound traffic and projects come from here.

The 48h Guide to a Personal Website

There's two things you need to figure out to create a personal website: what you want to communicate, and how you will communicate it. The best way we've found to get a jumpstart is to create version one of your site within 48 hours. Putting this time constraint in place forces you to focus on getting something out there and not succumbing to procrastination.

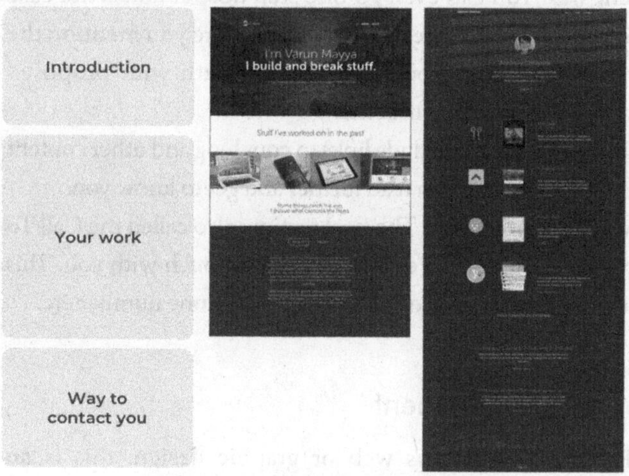

The three essential sections your website needs to have, with screenshots of our personal sites

I get it; you want to put the best impression out there for potential clients and anything sub par doesn't do justice to your skills and personality. But recognize that your quest for the perfect website will get in the way of having a website at all.

Content

Start with a pen and paper, and write down what you want to communicate. The three sections you need to focus on are:

Introduction: As soon as someone lands on your page, what is the first thing the need to know to set context for the rest of the site? This is your opportunity to sell yourself and set the right impression. It usually involves your name, what you do and what your skills are or just a bio. You can get creative here and experiment to find out the best way to communicate.

Your work: Show samples of your work and talk about what you did for that project. If you worked on the back end for an app, talk about the app, the challenge you faced and how long the engagement was. You can even go one step deeper and write case studies for each of your successful projects, where you mention the problem statement, how you approached it with your proposed solution and what was the outcome.

It is also a great idea to include links to your blog and other content in this section to get people to read further and get to know you.

The way to contact you: The final section, also called the Call To Action or CTA should be an easy way to get in touch with you. This can be your email address, a contact form, your phone number etc.

Design and Development

If your Pyjama Category is web or graphic design, this is an additional great way to showcase your skills. If not, that's okay too, you have a couple options to create one quickly.

Webflow/Squarespace: This is an amazing web design tool that you can use if you're a designer but don't want to hand code your site. They also have templates you can use. These two options let you buy domain and hosting along with making the site too.

webflow.com
squarespace.com

Bootstrap/Wordpress themes: There are some great free and paid themes that you can customize with your content and host online.

Web hosting and domain

A domain name is the address clients will enter into their browser to access your site. Web hosting is the server that will serve your web page to their browser. Pick a domain name that is easy to remember and type. We've picked abhinavc.com and varunmayya.com, you can pick what you like depending on availability. You can buy the domain on a domain registrar service like Namecheap or Godaddy for an annual fee.

How Do People Find It?

Be sure to include the link to your personal website everywhere people might discover you. This includes your Upwork profile and also your Twitter, Facebook, Quora, Medium, email footer and so on.

Posting your website to social networks is the best way to get people to visit it. But, keep in mind that doing so just with the expectation of getting views can get too self-promotional Creating new content is a way of creating new touch point that will eventually lead back to your site.

For example, a blog post you write might get a lot of views, and some people might in turn check out your website.

Promoting your content

The most obvious way to promote your content or website is to post to HackerNews, Reddit, Quora, Facebook, Facebook groups, Twitter and other places where it can get discovered. But relying only on this will lead to two things:

1. **Saturation:** Your Facebook friends will click the first few links and then stop. And that's okay; they're not your target audience anyway.
2. **Spam:** Posting your own stuff on HackerNews and Reddit every week will either get you banned from the subreddit or gather negativity in the comments for self-promoting.

So what do you do instead?

Whenever you are posting your own content, be mindful of the rules of the community you're posting in. Some are open to self-promotion, but others will ban you immediately.

Try to join the communities and make your voice heard. Genuinely contribute to discussions, questions from other members and things people need help with. When someone asks a question, help them out and link to your own content only when it is relevant. Use these topics of discussion to come up with content ideas to work upon.

The second step is to convert casual readers into a dedicated, recurring audience. Offer them a reason to sign up for your email list and use this to send them new content regularly. Without an email list, it's like you're hitting the refresh button on your audience and starting from zero every single time you post something new. Social media helps with audience building too, but it's not as powerful as email because social updates are usually seen only by

10% of your followers depending upon the time of day and how news feed algorithms work. Email, on the other hand, can have open rates of up to 70% and is a 1:1 way of reaching out to your audience.

Let's recap. The right way to build a personal brand is:

1. Work on enough projects and gain references to be notable in your field.
2. Create a personal website, Wordpress or a Medium blog.
3. Post original content that you've written on a regular basis. Pick a regular schedule, and stick to it, whether it's daily, weekly or monthly.
4. Build a recurring audience by creating a newsletter and sending out emails with this content.
5. Once you have more inbound projects coming in than outbound, you can wean off freelancing platforms and use them as only a secondary source. In the freelance community, you have now "**made it**".

Chapter 8
The Art of the Cold Email

"You do whatever, and I mean whatever it takes to get a potential client on a call. Then you do whatever it takes to close them."

—Alex Gonzales

Cold to warm

Building a pipeline of projects by investing in your personal brand is a great option. But sometimes that might not be enough, and you might want to do better and take matters into your own hands, rather than wait for clients to reach out to you.

This is where your outbound strategy comes in. There are millions of freelancers who probably do the same things as us. How is it that some make money and get recognized, but many are struggling for clients? How do you use outbound strategies to keep a steady pipeline of client leads coming your way after Upwork?

Both of my questions were answered last year when I met one of the smartest salespeople I've come across in a long time—Alex Gonzales. Now Alex works for a multi-billion dollar company and we met on a forum for software tools on the social network, Reddit. Eventually we got talking about working together on a new idea, a sales tool for entrepreneurs like you and me. During that conversation, he taught me a very cool technique that several salespeople use on an everyday basis that I was missing out on. It uses a combination of tools and methods to achieve results, but when we put it into practise on some of the businesses we were running, I was astonished by how well it worked.

Sales is an integral part of the freelance game. If you can't make a sale, it doesn't matter how good your technical skills are. You'll never land clients and you'll get demotivated very quickly. So I'm going to lay out the exact technique used by every single successful software/services company out there, right here in this book. You don't need another digital sales guide if you've absorbed this.

The general process of closing a sales prospect works something like this:

1. You find a list of prospects that might be interested in your freelance services.
2. You find their emails.
3. You send them personalized emails (or a generic email that seems like it's been personalized).
4. You hop on a call with the potential client if they reply to your email.
5. You figure out (depending on their purchasing power, their requirements and your financial status) if there's an opportunity to work together.
6. You close a deal and sign a contract that you will provide to the client.

What you're actually doing is sending out cold emails to relevant potential clients and turning some of those cold prospects "warm", that is, you're trying to form a connection with these potential clients. You're not selling up front, but rather having a chat with the prospective client on how you guys could potentially work together.

Let's run over each step one by one. They've worked so many times both for me and others who have used these techniques that it just doesn't make sense to me that there are people out there who don't use them at work.

Step 1: Prospecting

To send out cold emails, we're going to have to generate a relevant list of prospects. If you just send emails to thousands of people that have no connection to what you're doing, then you risk being marked as a spammer and having your email id banned. We don't want to spam people; we want to find clients who we can form a personal connection with.

For what we're about to do, you need an account on the social network for professionals, LinkedIn. After logging in to LinkedIn, you click on the Sales Navigator tool and activate a one-month subscription (it's free for the first month). Once you enter your details, click on the top right link, the Sales Navigator button. If you are a freelancer working in any of the Pyjama Categories, you want a prospect list that has decision makers of small-to medium-sized businesses that need your help. On Sales Navigator, key in the following details using the search function:

Demographic: United States (For this experiment, we're going to target a country with a high Big Mac index.)

Industry: Marketing and Advertising, internet, Events Services, Information Technology and Software

Title: VP, CXO, Partner

Company Size: 20–1,000 employees (Any lower than 20 employees and the company probably cannot afford you yet. Any more than 1,000 employees and the company is too big for you to quickly close a freelance gig. It takes months to close a big company on a freelance gig – there's better use of your time.)

Hit the Search button and wait for a relevant list of leads to show up. Now create a new excel sheet with the following structure:

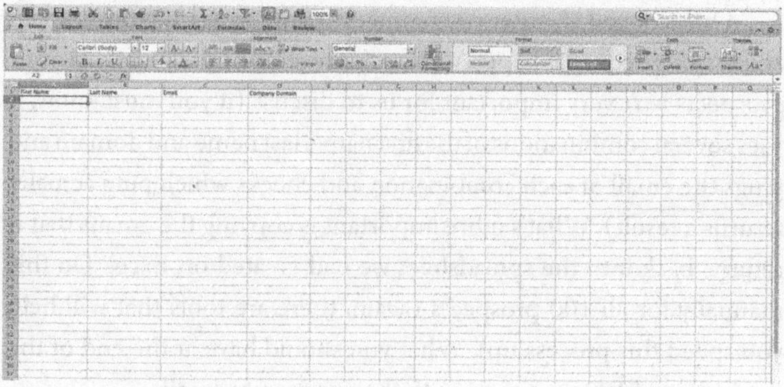

The supplementary skill of data entry comes into play here.

One by one, we're going to record the first name, last name, and company domain (eg: Microsoft.com) of each person we found on the LinkedIn search. For now, leave the email id blank. We're going to use a very smart tool to figure out each person's email id.

Fill in at least 100 rows so you don't have to keep doing this again and again. There are several tools out there that speed up the task of saving details from LinkedIn to Microsoft Excel, but for now, we're going to do it manually.

Step 2: Finding Emails

If you've followed Step 1 successfully, you now have a list of 100 decision makers from various companies across the United States. What we're going to do now is find their emails using a tool that I stumbled upon in the initial days of Jobspire. To do this, we need to use EmailMatcher (http: / / emailmatcher.com/). There are several tools that do what EmailMatcher does, but for the purpose of this book, we're going to stick to this one.

Sign up on EmailMatcher using your corporate email. Remember that part where we told you to make your personal website? Make sure it comes with an email id and use that one—EmailMatcher doesn't let you use a personal email like Gmail or Yahoo.

Once logged in, enter your contact's name and company domain and watch the magic happen. How the tool finds the emails of your prospects isn't very important for us to discuss (if you must know, it tries several combinations of the first name, last name and domain and pings the email of each combination and checks which ping actually returns a result). What's more important is copying the emails that it returns back into the spreadsheet we had created on Excel. Do this manually for all 100 prospects (again, there are tools that will help you speed this process up). What you should have at the end of the day is a list of 100 prospects, with their corporate emails.

Step 3: Sending Personalized Emails

This step is simple—you send over an email that the recipient will **want** to read. While simple in theory, it is extremely hard to figure out what your **recipient** likes. Lucky for us, we've got Google on our side! Since you have the first name, last name and company, you can actually find out relevant information about each person by simply dumping the three into Google. Here's an example of what copy pasting a column with data about me would return:

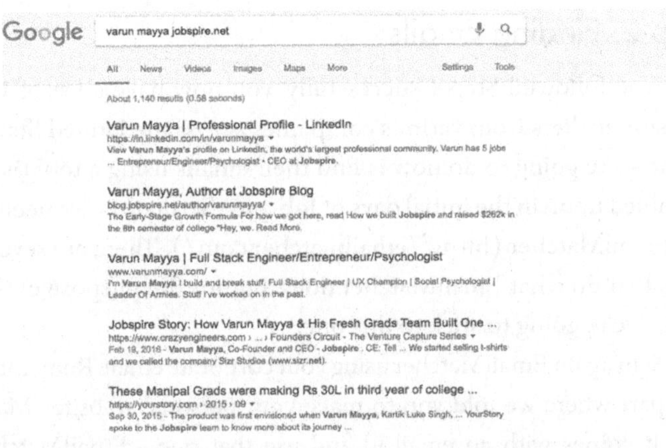

Sample search results when you Google a lead's name

Off the bat, you can see certain keywords that might be useful while sending me a cold email. Let's focus on "**Psychologist**" for now. While salespeople spend a lot of time doing research about a prospect, we're going to use a smarter technique—this time using Google News.

What we're going to do is type the keyword "**psychology**" into Google and hit the News tab.

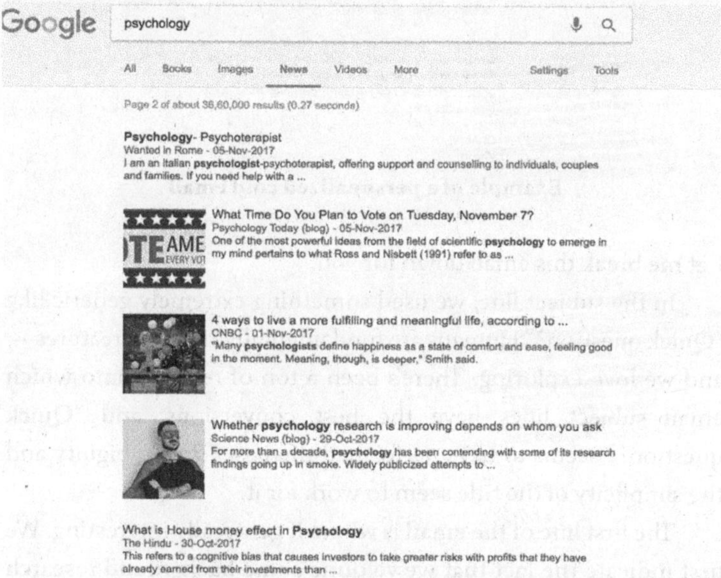

Type a keyword and navigate to the Google News tab

We're looking for something to form a connection with our prospect. Look at the third link—"4 ways to live a more fulfilling and meaningful life". In sales, we use any interesting articles, news pieces or even trivia to get a conversation going. Here's how I'd draft an email if I were emailing me.

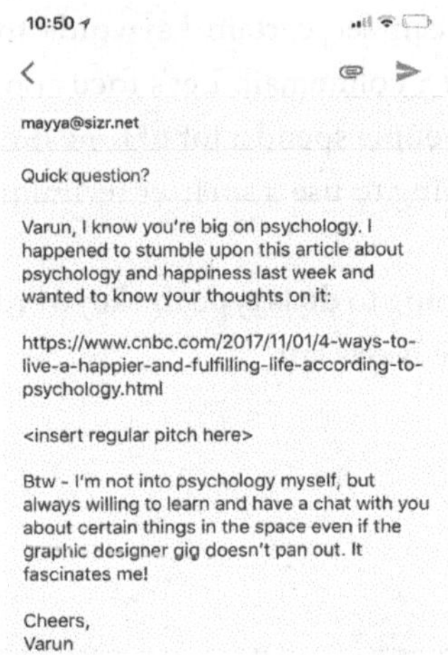

10:50

mayya@sizr.net

Quick question?

Varun, I know you're big on psychology. I happened to stumble upon this article about psychology and happiness last week and wanted to know your thoughts on it:

https://www.cnbc.com/2017/11/01/4-ways-to-live-a-happier-and-fulfilling-life-according-to-psychology.html

<insert regular pitch here>

Btw - I'm not into psychology myself, but always willing to learn and have a chat with you about certain things in the space even if the graphic designer gig doesn't pan out. It fascinates me!

Cheers,
Varun

Example of a personalized cold email

Let me break this email down for you.

In the subject line, we used something extremely generic like "Quick question?" Humans are fundamentally curious creatures—and we love exploring. There's been a ton of research into which email subject lines have the best conversions, and "Quick question?" seems to have performed the best. The ambiguity and the simplicity of the title seem to work for it.

The first line of the email is where it gets really interesting. We first indicate the fact that we've done some background research about the prospect. We then link them to a recent, relevant news article and ask them for their thoughts on it. Asking questions is always a good habit. Most people you email probably get anywhere between 10 to 10,000 emails a day, mostly about work! We make sure the email starts with a topic that has nothing to do with work, yet stimulates the prospect enough to take notice (people tend to notice what they already like or are interested in).

In the second paragraph, we let the prospect in on the real reason we sent them the email. Remember that pitch we made back on Upwork? We're going to plug that in the place that says "<insert regular pitch here>" in your email body. This part will be the same regardless of who you're sending an email to.

Finally, we end the email like a good sport. We tell the prospect we don't really know too much about the topic you started out talking about (unless you do, then mention something about it like would with a friend) and that you'd be willing to learn and have a chat about it, even if the prospect isn't interested in your graphic design services.

If a client ever rejects you for your graphic design skills but wants to talk to you about the topic you initiated take the call! You never know what can come out of a good conversation. I've had clients who weren't really interested in my skills end up referring me to their friends. One final thing about human beings—at the core, we want to help people we like. Same goes for every single person you're cold emailing.

Another high converting email that I use is the "friendly wager" email that I learnt from Alex. It works extremely well if you know the recipient is a sports fan. All you need to do is find that person's twitter or biography and figure out which sport they like and what their favorite team is. Here's how it goes:

Subject: Friendly Wager—Manchester United/Arsenal

Varun,

I noticed on Twitter that you liked Manchester United. Rather than me sending you an uncreative intro e-mail, I thought I would propose a friendly wager.

Man U is playing Arsenal this weekend (Soccer). I assume you will take United, so I will take Arsenal for the win. If United win, I will send you some football gear and if somehow Arsenal wins, then you will agree to take a 30 minute phone

> *call with me to learn more about how my graphic design skills add value to your company.*
>
> *Do we have ourselves a deal?*
>
> *P.S: I've attached my portfolio if you'd like to take a look at my skill set anyway.*

It seems counter-intuitive to send a mail so informal to someone you don't know. The reason this email works is because most of the people you send an email to get thousands of emails a day. The subject line of this email stands out and is extremely clickable not only because it doesn't seem sales-y, but because the recipient can relate to the topic (soccer). It shows that you've done your research, you understand their interests (in this case their favorite team) and the informal style of the email doesn't put your 'ask' out there until the very end.

Now it's your turn. Send a personalized email to all 100 prospects. It's time consuming and you might HATE doing it, but it's critical to your success. I see a lot of smart young people come up to me and say they like doing sales. At the very beginning of my career these were the kind of sales reps I used to hire. Over the next four years though, I realized how dead wrong I was about what it takes to be good at sales. Sales is less about smart and more about determined. Today, when I meet a potential sales representative, I ask myself just two questions.

1. Can this person follow our script?
2. Can this person send 100 personalized email or do 100 calls every single day; day after day, without losing motivation or energy?

Sales is all about repetition. You have to do the same thing over and over again. You have to face rejection almost all the time and still get up the day next day to start emailing and calling with a smile on your face. It's tough, but only the tough survive. Lucky for freelancers like us, we only have to do sales when we run out of projects—which means in time as you build a brand, rarely.

Step 4: Converting Replies to Calls

Let me give you some stats from my own experience. Out of every 100 emails you send, you should expect around 1% to reply. If you sent out all your emails, you should expect to get just 1 reply. Typically, an interested client might reply with a time or ask you some follow up questions. Share your phone number or Skype details and try to get them on a call as soon as you can. The longer it takes for the call to happen from the client's first reply, the higher the chances you will lose your project. Humans make decisions on impulse so it's important for you to get on a call as soon as possible, while your email is still fresh on their minds.

Step 5: Finding Opportunity on a Call

In the business world, the only thing that can lead to opportunity is conversation. Once you get on a call with a client, be genuine and upfront about your experience level and your interest toward the prospect's company. Be friendly and try to make conversation about things outside of business.

When I get on a call with a client, I try to make the call exciting. Most people in business have very boring conversations; so it's critical you make yourself out to be someone who is fun to with! It could be something as simple as talking about the latest news around the prospect's location or Trump's election or absolutely anything under the sun other than work!

During the call, try finding places you can help out with and try to let the client know you're a responsible and accountable freelancer. When the client explains their business, try to listen carefully so you can find synergy between what you do and what they do. This isn't an interview—you can find opportunity if you listen closely enough.

Step 6: Closing a Freelance Contract

A contract is an agreement between two parties that has legal binding. In other words, it makes sure you make your money and the client gets their services in exchange. Here is a sample freelance contract for designers that I recommend to new freelancers:

https://www.hellobonsai.com/freelance/sample-freelance-contract

A good contract will cover a lot of ground with very few words. Simply looking up "freelance contract" on Google will return a handful of contracts that might be useful to you. I would recommend hiring a lawyer and having them run through what each of those terms mean. For simple contracts, I actually think it's a good idea for you to read through it yourself and understand every detail. It's very important for a freelancer to have basic legal and financial intelligence and a simple contract is a good way to learn. The next chapter is a good intro to managing tax and contracts.

Send a signed contract over to your client, have them sign it (you can simply type in your name—many of these small contracts don't require handwritten signatures) and send it back to you. Now you can work for your client, anxiety free!

Prospecting and sending out cold emails are a brilliant way for you to create your own pipeline of projects. Being great at sales simply means being great at making conversation. It isn't hard to learn and is critical to your evolution as a freelancer.

Chapter 9

Tackling Tax

"The hardest thing to understand in the world is the income tax."

—Albert Einstein

What in the world is tax and why should I care?

Whether you're a full-time employee looking to freelance or coming straight out of college, this is probably a very important chapter for you. There are many types of tax, but we're going to talk mainly about income tax. While we've kept this chapter India specific, you can find the tax slabs for your own country online.

The government does not have its own money. In very simple terms, you pay the government a percentage of your income to provide you with the following services:

- Medicare and Health
- Transportation and Roads
- Military and Police Protection
- Basic Education
- Research into Science and Energy

So every rupee you give the government will be allocated to something that they deem useful to the general public. Because these slabs change often, we haven't listed them here. Check Cleartax.in or another website to find your tax bracket.

As a freelancer, you probably have some expenses that help you do business. The first thing we're going to do is calculate your Gross income and your Net income.

a) **Gross Income**
One of the advantages we have as freelancers is our ability to receive all income as online payments. It is super easy to calculate gross income this way. The gross income is always calculated for a given financial year—from the 1 April of a year, to 31 March of the next year.

b) **Net Income**
Unlike an employee, you have some expenses when it comes to doing business. Whether this is spending on task management software or buying a phone for work, you can put this down as a "business expense" and save tax on it. Gross income minus expenses equals net income.

c) **Depreciation**
When you buy a phone or a computer, its value reduces over time. That means to say that wear and tear catches up with electronic gadget over its lifespan.

The amount of decrease in each item's value is termed as depreciation. Photographers, for instance, can calculate the depreciation accumulated towards cameras, tripods and printing equipment they own. Web developers can denote depreciation towards laptops, time-tracking software and other devices they use.

Remember, depreciation is an economically beneficial way of spreading the cost of a given asset over a period of time, rather than showing expense upfront.

Filing Tax

Filing tax as a freelancer is fairly easy—you use the ITR (Income Tax Return) 4 form while filing your returns. Also, if your income is more than ₹ 1 crore, your account books need to be audited according to ITR laws, before 31 of September.

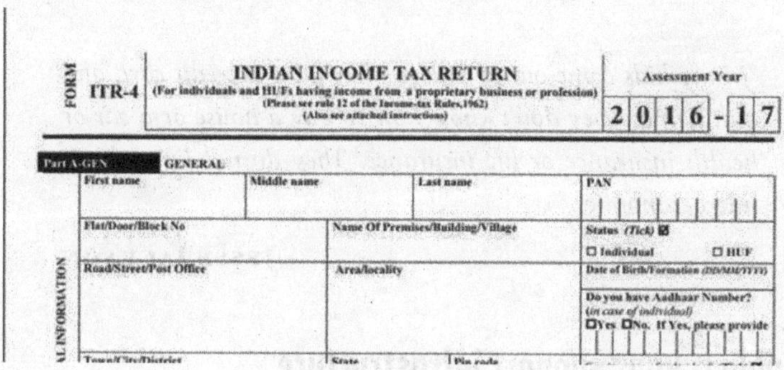

FORM ITR-4
INDIAN INCOME TAX RETURN
(For individuals and HUFs having income from a proprietary business or profession)
(Please see rule 12 of the Income-tax Rules,1962)
(Also see attached instructions)
Assessment Year 2016-17

Part A-GEN GENERAL

First name | Middle name | Last name | PAN
Flat/Door/Block No | Name Of Premises/Building/Village | Status (Tick) ☒ ☐ Individual ☐ HUF
Road/Street/Post Office | Area/locality | Date of Birth/Formation (DD/MM/YYYY)
Do you have Aadhaar Number? (in case of individual) ☐Yes ☐No. If Yes, please provide

Part of a sample ITR form

However, if your turnover is less than ₹ 1 crore, you don't need an audit and you can wait until 31 of July. Remember that a lot of this information is subject to change as tax rules change.

Chapter 10

Managing Your Finances

"Many kids come out of college, they have a credit card and a diploma. They don't know how to buy a house or a car or health insurance or life insurance. They do not know basic microeconomics."

—Jesse Jackson

Building your support infrastructure

One immediate, major drawback to freelancing is the lack of a support infrastructure. In a stable job, your employment probably includes at least basic health insurance, allowances, disability benefits, housing (sometimes) and a savings corpus.

In this chapter, we're going to talk about a topic I ask people who are starting their careers to take very seriously, something that most people find boring and have no inclination towards. We're going to talk about managing your finances. This will probably be the most boring chapter in this book after the chapter on tax, but this again is very important for life in general. This is meant to be a personal perspective and not investment advice; so please do your own research into what works best for you.

Many people, especially those fresh in the workforce, have absolutely no clue on how to effectively use their money, and this chapter is a crash course in making money work for you. I'm also giving you an insight into how to protect yourself in case of an accident, emergency or disability without you having to put too much money up front.

I learnt much of my personal finance skills from my co-founder at Avalon Labs, Shashank. At some point, we hope to write a longer thesis on managing money at the start of your career, but for now I'm going to create some simple financial rules. You might have heard the saying "money makes money". This couldn't be any truer. The magic of compound interest and mutual funds can only be experienced, not described. There are a plethora of ways you can lock your money up and have it make more money for you, and we're going to have a diversified portfolio that balances out risk and reward. Managing your finances is often complicated; so I'm going to make it as simple as possible. This guide is useful not just for freelancers but also for people in corporate jobs (you can skip the health insurance, though).

The first thing we're going to do is split our available capital in three ways:

– Savings and health insurance fund (35% of your after tax income)
– Monthly spend (25% of your after tax income)
– House rent and subscriptions like gym, Netflix, Apple Music, etc. (15% of your income)
– Experiment and learning fund (10% of your income)
– Splurge fund (15% of your income)

Let me quickly break this down for you and how to structure it. My suggestion is to have multiple savings accounts with banks. Some people don't even know they can open multiple bank accounts!

Almost every private bank in India allows you to create multiple accounts to section your funds. You should create four bank accounts.

a) Business account
b) Savings account
c) Monthly spend, house rent + subscription and experiment account (all three can be in one account)
d) Splurge fund account

Let's talk about each in a little more detail

a) **Business account:** As a freelancer, money should always be sent to your business account. Whether you take payments from your clients via Upwork, Paypal or direct bank transfer, you want to make sure it's this account the money is wired into. From a tax standpoint, it's easier to manage all incoming payments when they're arriving in one account.
b) **Savings account:** There are many ways to save money, but I'll quickly tell you what has worked for me. I've done considerable research on the topic and I'd advise you to do the same, but this is a broad overview of what you need to know.
   a. **ELSS:** The Indian government encourages you to save some money. Investments in tax-saving mutual funds, also known as equity-linked savings scheme (ELSS), qualify for tax benefits. Tax-saving mutual funds invest in the stock market and a bunch of other assets. They are geared toward investors with medium-to high-risk appetite. Because you are probably young and have time working in your favour, it makes sense for you to invest a proportion of our savings in a slightly high risk fund. Remember, investments are locked in for three years, but that's a good thing. Investments towards tax-saving mutual funds are tax free up to a maximum of ₹ 1.5 lakhs. Since we're going to investing in multiple tax-saving funds, we're going to aim

to save up to ₹ 1 lakh in ELSS and the minute you hit that value in any financial year, lock it in!

b. **NPS:** The New Pension Scheme is for people looking to set aside a retirement fund. You're probably in your twenties thinking about what the value of setting up a retirement fund is. Like I mentioned before, I've realized it's almost impossible to see a future you cannot comprehend. There might be a day where you want to call it quits, but cannot because you don't have enough money saved up. If you're above 18 years old, putting at least ₹ 50,000 in NPS is a good idea. Remember, the aggregate total of tax-free savings for NPS and ELSS is ₹ 1.5 lakhs; so our above split is perfect. Not only are we saving money, we're also saving on tax.

c. **Health Claim/Mediclaim:** An individual Mediclaim is one where you cover yourself against the financial liabilities of landing in a hospital. If you meet with an accident or fall sick, a Mediclaim corpus will cover your treatment. No human is infallible, but our ability to take precautionary measures is what makes us one of the smartest creatures on the planet. There are also some tax deductions to doing a Mediclaim up to ₹ 15,000—an added bonus.

It might also make sense to buy a "Family Floater"—something that insures your immediate family against hospitalization costs, but since this is a very simple savings model, I'm going to skip it.

You might notice how I've not put any life insurance in this plan; neither have I mentioned any particular policy to pick. In reality, you will need a life insurance plan at some point in your life, but I believe (and I know there are varying opinions on this topic) that you can skip it until you hit 30 or get married. It makes more sense to save a higher corpus into life insurance at a later point in life rather than block out a big part of your income right now that you should rather spend on learning new skills and making real money.

I also haven't picked a particular policy or a vendor yet because it really doesn't matter. Most ELSS, NPS and Mediclaim plans from different providers/vendors are very similar; just go with whatever makes most sense to you. I would also recommend you open a demat account and invest in stocks manually, but this is a simple financial model, so we're going to skip that part.

c) **Monthly spend account:** At the beginning of the month, have a standing instruction on your business bank account and have 25% of after tax funds moved here. Link this account to a spending app on your phone like Walnut to track recurring spends. You might own a gym subscription or use Netflix often. You need to keep track of these expenses, along with bigger expenses like your house rent, stepping out for dinner, etc. In the past I used to recommend getting yourself a credit card for this account (to improve your credit score and take loans later), but my controversial stance on this is that these days I think that's a bad idea.

The world around us is an increasingly distracting place. There are many things you can be tempted to buy with money you don't have. As you move up the freelance game, it becomes easier and easier to spend more out of this account guilt-free. After all, the entire point of this account is to try and go broke (we're smart enough to have other accounts that do the actual saving)!

Within this account, I've also mentioned a learning/ experiment fund. I encourage everyone to spend money on improving their craft (and learning other ones). Abhinav and I both constantly spend on new software and courses.

I like keeping up with Game Design theory even though I don't make games and Abhinav always keeps up with design.

d) **Splurge fund account:** Don't be fooled by the name of this account. This account will double as a "rainy day" fund if you're doing badly as a freelancer and a car/house/Euro trip fund if you're doing well. Just like your savings account, you aren't allowed to touch this money for a while.

   Remember what we said about goal setting? Suppose you have a goal of buying a car that costs ₹ 4 lakhs in two years. You need to make sure you save up enough for it first, right? That is exactly what this fund does. However, the magic with this fund is that in case you lose a big project and don't have enough money to put in your savings account or your monthly spend account, the Splurge fund account doubles up as your backup. **Every month, until you land another project that resuscitates your Business account, you withdraw money from the Splurge fund into your Savings and Monthly spend accounts.** If you do manage to land a project, then you can continue saving money into the splurge account as you would normally do from the next month. In time, you will have enough of a corpus to make a big purchase!

   I personally call this the motivation account. It motivates you to keep landing projects and stay cash flow positive so you can buy that dream car or that dream house, but also doubles up as a backup account when things go bad. Two birds, one stone.

Some more rules to remember:

1. **Avoid debt:** There is no better way for me to say this. Once you start freelancing and making some money

there is a temptation to spend, whether it is buying a new car or a new house. Think hard about your purchases and only spend planned amounts from the Splurge fund. Whenever you buy something that costs a lot but is in actuality just an upgrade, pre-plan it. Never buy a car or a house on impulse even if you have the money, ever.

2. **Talk about money:** For some weird reason, it's taboo to talk about money in India, even though it's an integral part of society. Have foundational conversations about money with your parents and significant other. Whether it is how much you're saving or understanding the value of a rupee this is critical to understanding finance. I personally believe that a person should have done freelance, as well as hired someone, at some time in their career. This teaches people the time value of money and how a certain number of hours of a person's time equals an iPhone or how many hours of work you have to put in to afford one liter of petrol. When you "get it", you'll realize how this imaginary concept called the market automatically balances the price of various resources depending on demand and supply—whether it be human labour or the price of a potato.
3. **Diversify:** As your savings grow over time, **where** you invest your money becomes more significant. Make sure you are investing in a diversified way. Spread your risk among large and small companies, across exchanges. It's tempting to put money into cryptocurrency, but the government seems to be on the fence about it, so I'd skip for now—although understanding the technology behind blockchain and smart contracts is a good idea regardless. Putting all your money in what you hope to be the next home run can leave you with a big hole in your savings.

4. **Habituate to a frugal lifestyle:** It's actually very easy to live a frugal, healthy lifestyle in India. The lower your personal "burn rate" (the amount of money you spend on yourself every month), the more money you can put into learning new things and trying out new and creative ideas. It's entirely possible to buy a Ferrari off your splurge fund (as long as it was pre-planned) and live on under ₹1,000 a day.

Chapter 11

Managing Stress and Ambiguity

"Adopting the right attitude can convert a negative stress into a positive one."

—Hans Selye

The hardest part of freelancing for most people isn't a technical concern, it's an emotional one. In a stable job, you never have to worry about where your next pay cheque is coming from, unless you're about to be fired. It's low stress, but there's also a cap on how much you can make.

In this section I'm going to tell you of my personal struggles with the stress and ambiguity of doing something all on my own. I'm rarely stressed these days not because I'm used to doing new things all the time (of course that helps), but because stress itself has no meaning or control over me—I'm simply desensitized to ambiguity in general. Abhinav and I have had multiple conversations about this. At some point in your career, failure will not matter to you. We don't know **when** this happened to us, but we know it happened around the same time—around four years into our freelance/entrepreneurship careers. At this point, everything you do is a "project" and it really doesn't matter if a project or two sink. But getting to this point is difficult, and I'm going to try to briefly describe how to deal with the ambiguity and stress of being a freelancer and getting to that point.

Don't take it too seriously

A lot of people will stress on the importance of having one (or multiple) of the following in your life:

- A stable job with a stable salary
- A nice house and a nice car
- Getting good grades
- Getting into a top-tier college or doing a PhD
- A stable marriage

First, here are some facts: The modern human evolved around 200,000 years ago. Compared to that, the first house came up 12,000 years ago and the concept of modern paper money only came into effect just 1,000 years ago. The first modern university was established just 300 years ago!

What I'm trying to say is that these concepts of what makes a person "successful" have existed for only a small fraction of our history as humans. It's astounding how seriously some people take these concepts. There are young children being forced into studying for college at the age of 12 only to find out in their thirties that they've missed out on a fun and healthy childhood. The world is an incredibly complex system which consists of several smaller systems that somehow manage to work in tandem. Most importantly, these systems are disrupted every single day.

Fifteen years ago, there was no Facebook, Whatsapp, Instagram, Upwork, LinkedIn or Snapchat. When these technologies came in, they broke the foundations of how we communicate. We started seeing people change their lifestyles rapidly to become respected or liked in their online circles while disregarding their actual interests. We started seeing people cancel their cable subscriptions just to be overwhelmed by the plethora of choices available on Netflix. The game has changed everywhere, so why do we still take metrics that were once important in the previous generation like having a stable job and good grades seriously?

Let me tell you from my experience at Jobspire why good grades are important: When a big recruiter wants to hire people, they typically get hundreds of thousands of CVs a month. They would love to interview each person individually, but it's simply too exhausting to sift through so many CVs. Using a GPA (grade point average) system helps them pick the top few CVs without having to interview that many people. Colleges are designed to put you up against deadlines all the time, simulating what it would be like when you start working at a large company. GPA in most colleges is a good measure of how well someone can follow instructions and how hard someone can work, plain and simple.

From experience, recruiters in India make the final hiring decision based on gut feel rather than using a solid metric, regardless of how many tests they put the candidate through. Even to massive companies, your ability to learn and your attitude are more important than your GPA. GPA is simply a filtering system and it's been around for a very short time considering how long humans have walked the Earth.

Similarly, it made a lot of sense in the past to buy a house because it seemed like a long term investment. Today, with economies of scale and rent rates, you will have to live in one house for nearly 40–80 years to justify your investment. **Are you 100% sure you will live in the same place for the next 40–80 years,** considering the number of opportunities and globalization that airplanes and the internet have brought us?

Marriage is the final cornerstone of "success" that I'm going to dissect. Marriage was seen through most of history as a way to form strategic alliances between families, with the youngsters about to be forced into wedlock having no say in the matter. Until hundred years ago marriage didn't even consider men and women equal, with women and children being considered "property". Fewer people these days are considering getting married and more couples are choosing to cohabit. The rates of marriage in Europe decreased by 30% between 1975 to 2005. While I'm still on the fence about marriage, I still don't think it should be a metric of "success" like your uncles and aunts would have you think.

Because of the society we live in, we tend to take some things extremely seriously, whereas other, irreversible things, like taking care of your health, take a back seat.

How does freelancing play into this equation? With rising automation, I personally don't think there will be many non-start-up jobs around in 40 years. Why? Because most large companies want to automate (they're already doing it, FYI) most human tasks. At this point, the mechanical, one track concepts most corporate employees would have learnt will be useless. As Eric Hoffer observed, "In times of change learners inherit the earth; while the learnt find themselves beautifully equipped to deal with a world that no longer exists."

Freelancing is less about making some money now; it's more about gaining the ability to learn new skills, adapting to unstructured situations and being prepared for the future. Over the last seven years, I've learnt at least 40–50 new skills each year. Whether it be the ability to use Photoshop (I learnt that in year 1) or the ability to do my taxes (I learnt that in year 3). Both Abhinav and I have always been forced to learn new things. It isn't because we're particularly inclined or motivated to learn new things, it's because we have historically had **no choice**. When you're doing a project and a client says "You need to know X", you have two choices. The first option is you tell your client you don't know how to do X and risk losing the project or you say you already know how to do X and learn it on the fly. Abhinav and I have always taken the second option, and in almost every case, so has every other successful freelancer.

I don't freelance anymore, but I still maintain the attitude of learning things on the fly and never shying away from absorbing something new, however difficult it seems on the surface. Everything becomes easy with repetition, even if the first few days of learning something seem hard. Most people either don't know this or even after knowing, they haven't experienced it. I've been through it so many times that I expect confusion whenever I start doing anything new. I also know that with enough practice, the confusion disappears and the feeling of "flow" sets in. Every freelancer or serial entrepreneur knows this. It is extremely critical to adopt this mindset of "I can learn anything" whenever you're faced with any learning task—be it cooking or machine learning.

Remember this image from before? The fastest way to learn is to copy something and understand how it was made. There will be some initial confusion, but that will pass.

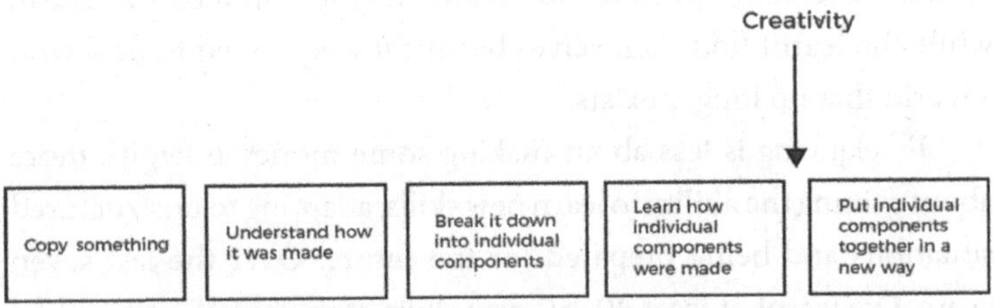

Where creativity plays into the equation of freelance work

Overcoming anxiety

If you ask most people in the world how to be successful, they're going to tell you to "focus". Unfortunately, recent research in psychology disagrees with this sentiment. The mind is a simulation machine. Say you have to deliver a presentation at 6 PM tomorrow. Even if you're fully prepared, the mind continually simulates this event in your head. A lot of people will commend you for staying focused on the event. You know what this is actually called though? **It's called anxiety.**

By its nature, the mind cannot stay focused; let no one tell you otherwise. This is why it's important to write very tangible goals on a piece of paper and avoid using your head to stay focused. Coming back to that public speaking event, it makes more sense for you to completely distract yourself until it's time to actually go on stage. Worrying is completely useless—there is not one single thing that worrying accomplishes. This is where distraction comes into effect. You simply don't think of the event until it's time for the event itself. In order to distract yourself, you need to find something outside of work you like doing.

Whether that's hanging out with funny friends, watching a movie, playing some music or playing a computer game, do whatever is necessary to avoid thinking about the stressful event. If my co-founder and I have a stressful event coming up, we typically fire up a game of online Overwatch or Dota and distract ourselves until the event.

The same thing applies to the ambiguities of being a freelancer. When will I land my next project? When will the client pay? Am I going to make it? We've been through some of these questions before, but it helps to distract yourself because some of these questions can't be answered at the moment and the brain enters loops that don't really answer the question but put you in "analysis paralysis". Sometimes, it's important to not think, but do, and this is one of those times. As long as you have a plan on paper, just defer any unanswered questions to a later time. Put faith in your abilities and hustle your way through to the other side.

The only times you should focus are when you are setting your goals, when you're learning and when you become aware that you are wasting **too much** time. Otherwise, it's all good fun—there's nowhere to go and let nobody convince you that you're running out of time.

Freelancing can be a tad bit harder on people who have a hard time with stress, ambiguity or anxiety, but there is no better feeling than the freedom you will have once you crack the formula for **your success** as a freelancer.

I'm going to leave you with this quote I found on Reddit a long time ago. It has nothing to do with the technical aspects of freelance, but getting good at the freelance game is 90% managing your expectations and anxieties, especially when it comes to dropping a full time job to do this:

> *Listen, become one with the anxiety. I promise you this, you will never understand anxiety if you have any kind of aversion to your experience. Anxiety is simply a certain energy that is labeled as do-not-want and it's sustained only by your labeling and complete misunderstanding of the energy. The energy that you have labeled anxiety can be the absolute best feeling in world, it can be pure excitement, it can be bliss. Instead of being so self-focused and seeking a certain feeling, take a step back and observe the energy you are experiencing, how does this energy relate to my thoughts, how does this energy relate to what I do, is there fear, fear of what, get to the bottom, go into the dark corners of your thoughts, what is the worst possible thing that can happen, look at it, is it real, does it have any reality of its own? I promise you this, no thought can harm you, no matter what you experience, it will pass, like everything else. Anxiety is the greatest teacher there is.*

Chapter 12
Robots Will Take Your Job

> *"There is no reason and no way that a human mind can keep up with an artificial intelligence machine by 2035."*
>
> —**Gray Scott**

Artificial intelligence (AI)

What's a chapter about AI doing in a book about freelancing? Well, simple statistics really. A report put out in February 2016 by Citibank in partnership with the University of Oxford predicted that **47% of US jobs are at risk of automation. In the UK, 35% and in China, it's a whopping 77%.**

According to research by Business Insider, three of the world's 10 largest employers are are now replacing their workers with robots.

Remember the Life cycle of a Skill graph from chapter three? A skill goes through the stages of **early adoption, acceptance, peak popularity, commoditization and then partial or complete automation.** Not only does this apply at a micro level to skills and sub skills but also at a macro level to jobs and industries.

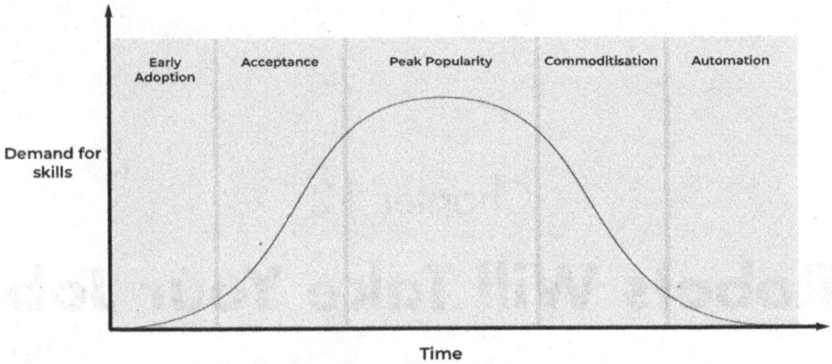

The Adoption Bell Curve applies at a macro as well as a micro level

Most jobs ripe for automation are repetitive tasks. This means jobs that people have been doing for years like manual labour, restaurant waiters or bank tellers are at the risk of being taken over almost entirely by a computer!

More and more traditional retail stores are shutting down because they just can't compete with their ecommerce counterparts, not because they are less popular, but because the costs of running a physical store and having employees show people around are several times more than running an e-commerce store. At the start of this century, maintaining an e-commerce store would cost you a minimum of $200,000 a year, whereas today it costs less than $30 a month for a Shopify account.

There are chat bots that are replacing aspects of customer support, are always nice to customers, are easy to fix and come at a one-time cost instead of having to be paid a monthly salary. Because anybody in the world can build a bot with tools available today. The cost of a bot is extremely cheap—every time someone builds a bot at a low price, someone outbids that person and builds an even cheaper bot in a quick bid to make more money. Humans can't be down priced like this (we have to buy groceries and pay rent); so these kinds of roles are becoming less viable options.

Should I be scared?

This might all sound like a futuristic dystopia, but it's real and it's around the corner. Being on the edge of recruitment has shown us data that's telling us that employers are avoiding hiring for repetitive roles—instead saving their money to hire senior talent. If there's something a bot cannot do, an employer would much rather hire a freelancer or an agency for the short term and get it done instead of taking on the liability of hiring someone full time. Executives who once relied firmly on their intuition and experience are now face-to-face with machines that can learn from massive amounts of data and make informed decisions like never before. Self-driving cars are already starting to entice customers and have much cleaner track records than real drivers!

When you take jobs away from people and remove their source of income, not only do they start having difficulties making ends meet, they also have a lot of time on their hands. These people are drawn towards self-destruction. The human mind needs creativity, social contact and freedom, but the human body needs food, clothing and shelter—all of which need money. A starving, idle group of people, especially in a country like India, eventually turn violent and this is a terrible, terrible idea of a future. Even if a universal basic income comes into play, it's still not going to change the fact that there's going to be a lot of people with no work. Humans have a mind that invents problems—real or fictional. If you're not solving a real problem, your mind will invent a fictional problem to keep you busy. Imagine that in large numbers!

How the Pyjama Economy helps

The Pyjama Economy removes all reliance on a stable salary. If you're fired or replaced by a machine at your full-time job, it would take you quite some time to find a new one or to learn the skills required to find a new job. All Pyjama Categories, except data entry, cannot be completely automated in the next 10 years at the least. Aside from that fact, all Pyjama Categories are all great for creative expression! So it can't just be used to make you some money, but also prevent boredom and idle time.

I cannot stress the importance of having creative outlets in a world that is becoming more connected but at the same time, more isolated. With automation, that isolation is going to increase and most of our interaction will happen online. Pyjama Categories will help you take your trade online and stay relevant over the next decade.

Those entering the Pyjama Economy and becoming a freelancer must find and pursue their own personal mission in life rather than strive to become a cog in the machine—playing a minor role in society to serve someone else's purpose.

In five years, college courses and other channels of higher education will be open to the public, online. To give you an example, I'm currently doing a course in Genetics and Genomics from Stanford and hope to complete it within three months. The point being that the resources for us to prepare for the coming AI revolution are available online. Some people will resist, but entering the Pyjama Economy will allow you to embrace that change and stay ready.

When each human being can create one unique combination of experiences and skills based on their personal interests and purpose, they can build their own unique brand story. The chapter "Creating your personal brand" in this book reflects that idea. This is the only way they can differentiate between themselves and a trainable machine—the trainable machine has no heart, no passion and no creativity (machines will get pretty creative soon though).

The herd is about to get a lot bigger, so step out right now and bring the world your unique flavour of passion, creativity and skill—join the Pyjama Economy today. I'll see you on the other side!

Freelancer to Entrepreneur

The Jobspire Story

"There's nothing wrong with staying small. You can do big things with a small team."

—Jason Fried

At some point in my career, I decided I was done with freelancing. I was hitting my targets so fast that I was making enough in one week to last me months. With that complacency came laziness and I actively avoided taking up new projects. At this point, Kartik and I chose to completely stop freelancing and work on something more meaningful—a full-blown start-up. We were still in college at that point, but started working on Jobspire, a recruitment platform.

Here's an excerpt from a story I had written on my blog—the story of how we raised funding while still in college; a story that has now been shared millions of times across the web and spent an entire day trending on Yahoo's front page.

Part One: Manipal

A year ago—I recollect the incident that started this madness.

"We're making quite a bit of money as students, dude," mused Kartik.

"Yeah, let's do something even more challenging. Let's do something big."

"What problem hasn't been solved yet?" asked Kartik.

"Let's do hiring, man. The biggest competitor in the market is living on borrowed time anyway; let's dethrone them."

"Sounds good."

And that was it. We shut SIZR down the very next day and began planning what Jobspire would look like a year into the future.

I immediately drafted a north star—a vision document. Something I'd show to our own employees to inspire them to work here.

Kartik and I had been working since the first year of college. We were really good product developers, but that wasn't enough—we needed to hire some more people. I remember there was an incredible rush because we were entering the fourth year of college. Everyone was looking for a "placement" and Tata Consultancy Services (TCS) was hiring en-masse. I needed to outsell the 100+ other companies appearing on campus to the people I thought I'd want to work with. I looked through my contact list and found Sandesh Kini—a quiet person who used to sit on my bench at the back of class.

College had closed for the mid-semester holidays and he lived in Bahrain. I asked him if we could Skype.

"What's up?" he said, in his usual nonchalant tone.

"Dude! Forget placements and come work with me. I have this start-up idea and we think we can revolutionize how work happens across the country. It's ambitious, but it could work."

"I'm in."

"What? Don't you want to ask your parents or take a while to think?"

"Nope! I'm in."

This is the fastest I've seen anyone commit to something which at that point was a career-defining risk. We didn't have the experience we have today, and Sandesh had absolutely no skills to contribute. Kartik and I used Ruby on Rails and a bunch of other technology. While Sandesh was a CS Engineer like us, he had no clue how Ruby worked—he had spent his time freelancing as a video designer.

"But I don't know Ruby or how to do any of this."

"I'll teach you."

"Sounds good," he said and he signed off.

A year ago, most people in this situation would've said "I have X number of job offers, why should I choose you?" but till today I'm impressed by his decision. Sandesh has transformed into one of the best product developers I know—and we meet product developers on a daily basis.

"Okay, so who's going to sell?" I asked.

"We'll need someone to sell, but we're in an engineering college," Sandesh quipped.

I looked through my contact list and found Mohak Dhingra, another quiet kid who I'd worked with at a student organization called AIESEC. He was my neighbour and we didn't interact much.

I walked straight to his house and said:

"Dude, come work with us. We're going to start-up."

"Huh? What's a start-up? I already have a job offer from Mu Sigma dude. Sorry".

Being the nice guy that he is, he apologized and shut the door. Being the not-so-nice guy that I am, I rang the bell again.

"Dude, think about it. It's a risk but it'll be fun. A few years later when someone writes a book about this, do you want to be the guy who rejected something as awesome as this?"

"I don't want to put my career on the line. Mu Sigma is a safe bet."

"Don't delude yourself. There's no such thing as safe."

After almost two hours of attempting to convince him, he cracked. "Okay, speak to my dad."

After a quick Skype session with Mohak's father, he was sold.

"This is the best time to take a risk," said his father.

Mohak agreed, but he still wanted to keep his Mu Sigma offer on hand. I said he could, but under the condition that he doesn't tell the rest of the team about it.

To me, it meant our team was complete. We had everything we needed to be self-sufficient and Kartik and I began working on a prototype for the product. With our old projects, we were such a good team that one person would choose to do the design and front end while the other person would do the back end. Kartik chose the back end; so I positioned myself on the design front. We needed someone to do the testing; so I spent eight hours everyday for almost a week teaching Sandesh how to write tests. Truth be told, he learnt much faster than me and put in a degree of effort I once thought was impossible.

We slogged away for three months. While Mohak was contacting every HR he could find asking them about their problems, Sandesh wrote the tests and Kartik and I wrote the code. We noticed we weren't getting much sleep. We had to attend college from 8 AM to 5 PM and then we'd work from 7 in the evening to 4 in the morning. I didn't even know when we slept or ate. It was pure adrenalin.

Work took a toll on us. Nobody could handle the physical and mental stress, being always on our feet and then sleeping three hours a day. Writing Jobspire code a day before my exam, I started to crack. I was starting to feel uneasy, random spells of shortness of breath and a general sense of gloom. So I went to see a doctor.

"You have a blood pressure of 160/100, your resting pulse is 100 and your serum cortisol (stress hormone) is 36 μg/dL," said the doctor.

"How do I fix it?"

"Go to Goa."

Stupid advice, I thought to myself. I don't need a vacation.

I've never been more wrong in my life.

It's incredibly hard to describe a panic attack. That evening, I felt strange and puked out the pieces of bread I ate. I suddenly felt very confused about where I was and what I was doing. My hands and feet were trembling and my breathing was fast. Now I'm not an idiot, and I know what hyperventilation can do to you. My hands and feet lost so much sensitivity that I wasn't able to clench my fists. My entire left side was hurting like hell. I thought I was having a heart attack and the ceiling was blurring fast. Sandesh, Kartik and my flatmate Tejus rushed me to a hospital.

The heart monitor showed that my heart rate was 160 and rapidly increasing.

"So this is it?"

For some reason, I was least bothered about dying. I was a little disappointed that I wasn't able to finish what I started, but I was so dazed, I just closed my eyes. The panic attack subsided in a few hours.

"What was that?" I asked the doctor.

"That's what happens when you take things too seriously".

I woke up the next morning, still feeling completely out of whack. I don't think I can ever function like this. I feared what I felt at that point was permanent. We were still in Manipal, so I took the first flight for home. I stayed at home for about a week. In that time, both my thought process and my mind returned to normal. It felt good to be back.

I took the next flight back to Manipal and appeared for my exams. The team got together, this time with a new addition. It was Rushil, a new developer who we'd hired. Sandesh had taken up the responsibility to train him; he was now a full-stack developer. It was the best piece of news I'd heard in months. I'd also been reading a lot to prepare myself for the journey ahead. Sandesh was in the same class, so he started reading a lot as well. We used to get kicked out of class often for reading books about start-ups, psychology, marketing, meditation and everything else under the sun.

During this period, we went to an event in Bengaluru where we met Anshumani Ruddra, who, at that point, was the head of Tiny Mogul Games (Hike Messenger's game studio) and one of our first mentors. It gave our team a little more exposure. I also made a bold move and hired Prajwal, a friend of mine from Bengaluru to come onboard as a co-founder. It was another easy sell.

Part Two: Delhi

The seventh semester of college was over. Everyone had found jobs and we were still building our product. "Guys, college is a big time suck. I don't want to do the eight semester. I think we should just drop out," I proposed.

Kartik agreed while Sandesh and Mohak looked at us with disbelief.

"You're asking us to waste the 3.5 years of effort? You think our parents are going to be okay with that?"

"Yeah," I said. I knew Kartik was with me because we'd gained enough experience and confidence to know that college was a waste of time. There was a dearth of developers and we were minting money. $100/hour was SIZR's average billing rate.

"There's got to be some other way out of this," said Rushil.

"Varun, game the system."

"How?" I asked

"Let's find an incubator or a company to work under. The eight semester can either be done in college or as an internship under some other company."

Technically, we were doing the most complicated internship ever, but we'd still need some company to take us under their wing.

My first instinct was to apply to Microsoft Accelerator. A few weeks later we got a mail saying that while we got into the top 10% of all applicants, we neither had the product nor the team to be considered.

"Screw that, let's look for others," I said optimistically, even though we were running out of time. As the CEO of the company, it was my job to sound optimistic all the time, even if I didn't feel optimistic at all.

We looked around and found a few good ones. Mohak came to us and told us that there was this great incubator in Delhi that one of his friends had worked with.

When we approached the incubator, we made it clear to them that this was an internship for us and freed up a lot of time instead of spending hours a day at college. While we could've done all of this in college, we had to spend four hours a day compulsorily in college without internet. I knew how to hack into the college internet and give me unlimited access, but we'd all be in different classes and it would be hard to coordinate.

"Delhi it is, guys."

While Rushil and Mohak were from Delhi and super happy about the decision, Sandesh was neutral and Kartik was visibly upset.

"Why Delhi, dude? It's going to be 5 degree Celsius and we don't have any friends there."

My logical reply to Kartik's question was a short one:

"YOLO."

Prajwal couldn't make it to Delhi (his college wasn't letting him leave), so I had to tell him that he couldn't be a part of this anymore. I felt like I let him down. I could let the emotion of letting someone go (especially a long-time friend) affect me, but I had to stay focused, at least for the rest of the team.

So off we went to Delhi. We logged on to Housing.com and failed to find a house. They were either already booked or the pictures/cost were misrepresented. We ended up wasting a week, then took a small three bhk apartment at Maple Heights in Sushant Lok, Gurgaon. We were paying 25k in rent and the four of us—Rushil, Kartik, Sandesh and I—were to live together while Mohak was to live with his parents in Delhi and come to work at 8 AM everyday.

Our apartment/office in Gurgaon

A makeshift tripod stand

A makeshift standing desk

The way we worked for the next three months DEFINED shoestring. My back was giving up, so we made a makeshift microwave standing desk. We used borrowed thermocol to make a video rig to explain the video resume part of our product. We were really crunched. In March, we had a complete product that looked and felt awesome. We were stressed and tired, but the product was finally completed. We decided not to do any PR or marketing.

"Let's just tell people," I said.

Mohak brought on our first few companies while the rest of us randomly spoke to people on LinkedIn asking them to use Jobspire. It was amazing to see a few people using the platform. We had 70 sign-ups that month. A year later, we had nearly 1,000 sign-ups a day—still spending nothing on marketing. Over 1,500 companies ended up using Jobspire.

To counter the stress from working hard and sleeping so little, we played all sorts of indoor games, from Pictionary to a weird version of indoor badminton to just sitting and telling each other our fears and goals in life. We were becoming family.

As we grew, we met investors. We couldn't keep burning the money we had made from SIZR. The first investor I met ran a famous media company. I had traveled nearly four hours to reach his place and I didn't have any clue on how valuation economics worked.

"What valuation are you looking at?" he asked, slowly sipping a cup of tea.

"I'm not sure," I said, thinking at the back of my mind that I'd have to go to Quora and check out what that meant.

"I don't want to invest cash in you, at least not entirely."

I was upset. We worked so hard and here's an investor telling us he's not going to invest cash.

After Anshumani, our mentor's advice, I read a lot about angel investing, deal metrics in India, etc. This was not before I embarrassed myself in front of several other investors. We were preparing for another pitch event (In my experience, these are useless. No deal happens on stage.), when Nikunj Jain and a few other investors happened to interview me on Skype. Nikunj absolutely loved the product.

"Yes, I'll invest," he said.

His confidence helped us through a particularly rough patch we were having. The minute he said he would put in some cash, the team suddenly stood up and hit fifth gear again. We haven't slowed down since that day.

Part Three: Bengaluru

At this point, we took a call and moved to Bengaluru. The weather in Delhi was horrible and we realized that we were still young and needed friends. Nobody in the team had gone out of the house for four months. Isolation can drive you insane. We made the switch to a place where we had friends and where the weather was calmer. I wasn't a believer in things like weather or environment affecting people—but here I was, wrong yet again.

It was at around this point when we met Ravi Srivastava from Purvi Capital. Initially, Ravi had committed ₹ 3 lakhs and wanted to take on a mentorship role, but we were really pushing the traction and we saw incredible growth spurts. Ravi was raising a fund at that point and he asked me if we'd like to be a part of his portfolio. I was an expert on deal metrics by then but I didn't even think about the valuation.

I'd realized that angel deals are not about the percentage you dilute or the valuation of the company, it's about the people you'd like to work with. We thought Ravi and Nikunj were awesome, self-driven people who thought like us, so we said yes. We got a pretty good (multi-million) dollar valuation at the end of it all. Towards the end, a lot of investors saw us as a good deal and everybody wanted to jump in and put in cash. We were very oversubscribed and had to make decisions on who to remove from the round!

A term sheet for ₹1.7 crores came through and while the paperwork took some time, we finally managed to raise a round and make sure we have amazing people involved.

We went on to hire over 20 new people, ex-Amazon, ex-Twitter and ex-Zomato employees, including people much older than us, and rented a decent office space in Ulsoor that we re-did ourselves to reflect our culture back in the old days. We even re-hired some of the people who we had to let go. The most impressive fact? At that point we didn't even have our degrees.

Businesses can fail at any time. There are just too many variables, some out of your control and some in your control. For us, this was never about the business. It was about family, and sticking together—through sadness, failure and success.

So why did I take us on a trip down memory lane? To tell you what freelancing really helped me do – take the plunge into starting up and play on the grandest stage of them all – the funded start-up game. But this isn't the only progression from being a freelancer.

The other alternative – building a smaller product start-up

Over the last few years, I've come to realize that there's another natural progression to freelancing—building and scaling a product. The math is simple. If you build something customers will pay $10 for every month, at 100 customers, that's an incoming monthly revenue of $1,000. If you scale up to 10,000 customers, you're suddenly making $100,000 a month!

Product Success Formula—**Charge something for a simple product * Sell it to enough customers**

People in the start-up world tend to overcomplicate the above math—they throw in buzzwords like valuations, innovation, freemium and thought leadership. But in essence the formula is simple—you sell more of something than is required to sustain you and the people that work with you. Buffer and 37 signals are great examples of companies that follow that simple formula—and do it very well. Passive income completely removes the need for you to work and according to me employees at companies like Buffer and Basecamp have the best quality of life compared to the crash and burn lifestyle of (almost every) VC-funded start-up.

You Can't Do It Alone

Whether it's a funded start-up or a small business, you'll need a team. My argument to running a company over personal freelancing has been simple—you need someone to take the load off you. There are times as a freelancer where you will be sick, or are handling too much. This is where a team will help you. Every digital business today requires at bare minimum just one person from each Pyjama Category—everything else can be outsourced.

Here's what you will need:

1. A product developer to lead the product
2. A UI/UX designer to figure out design and interaction (you can sometimes eliminate the need for a designer by using commercially available templates and themes)
3. A back-end developer
4. A website designer, also called a front-end developer (sometimes, a freelancer can be both a back-end and front-end developer, also called a "Full-Stack" developer)
5. A marketing person to do your digital marketing
6. A salesperson to scrape leads and send email sequences
7. An outsourced legal and CA consultant

With this team, you could build almost any Software as a Service (SaaS) tool out there right now. A SaaS tool is generally a software tool that is based on the cloud so that nobody needs to download, yet provides some value to a customer such that he or she pays some money for every month in "recurring monthly payments" You need to come up with a great idea to build, but with enough experience we're confident you can build great products that make passive income. However, you should be prepared for the possibility of your first few products failing.

Most freelancers end up building small remote teams and work on such tools. I've yet to meet a freelancer who has worked more than four years in his field and not started something of their own. The backbone and safety net that freelance gives you allows you to take some risks and if it works out, could make you sweet passive income.

Thank you for reading this book! To receive free updates and resources, join the Pyjama Profit community at pyjamaprofit.com

About the Authors

Varun is a computer science engineer from Manipal Institute of Technology who raised funding in India at the age of 20 for the recruitment platform, Jobspire. Since then, he has hired over 200 people and now runs the 40-man Avalon Labs, a profitable holdings company that owns multiple businesses and dabbles in edge technology like artificial reality, blockchain and AI.

Abhinav is a UI/UX designer with a degree in computer science from Manipal Institute of Technology. Starting out as a freelancer, he has worked with over 60 tech start-ups in India and Silicon Valley. Abhinav currently leads UI/UX design at Unacademy, a like-minded start-up in Bengaluru.